Fig. 23 Goya. "*A caza de dientes*" (núm. 12). *Los dientes y la grasa de los ahorcados son hechizos famosos.*

UNIVERSITY OF NORTH CAROLINA
STUDIES IN THE ROMANCE LANGUAGES AND LITERATURES
Number 62

THE GOLDFINCH AND THE HAWK:
A STUDY OF LOPE DE VEGA'S TRAGEDY,
EL CABALLERO DE OLMEDO

THE GOLDFINCH AND THE HAWK:
A STUDY OF LOPE DE VEGA'S TRAGEDY,
EL CABALLERO DE OLMEDO

BY

WILLIAM C. McCRARY

CHAPEL HILL
THE UNIVERSITY OF NORTH CAROLINA PRESS

Printed, 1968, in the United States of America

Garrett Press, Inc.
New York, N.Y.

*To my wife Sally Jane
in her quiet courage*

TABLE OF CONTENTS

PART I

1. Sources   15

2. Courtly Love   27

3. Alcahuetería and Brujería   51

PART II

Act   I   85

Act   II   100

Act   III   125

Bibliography   177

A Note to the Second Printing   183

ACKNOWLEDGEMENTS

I should like to express my most sincere gratitude to Professors Everett W. Hesse, of the University of Southern California, John E. Keller, and Alfred E. Engstrom, of the University of North Carolina, Vicente Cantarino, of the University of Indiana, Miss Nancy Kenington, Mr. Leon Lyday and Mr. Rupert Pickens, of the University of North Carolina, and above all to my wife for their encouragement, careful reading of my manuscript, and the many suggestions they made for its improvement. I also owe a debt to the American Council of Learned Societies and the American Philosophical Society, both of which provided funds for a summer's research in the Biblioteca Nacional de Madrid, and to the Research Council of the University of North Carolina whose generous grant more than met publication costs.

Chapel Hill, 1965

PART I

1. SOURCES

Students of the Spanish *comedia* have been puzzled, perhaps, by the surprising lack of analytical attention devoted to one of Lope de Vega's most arresting plays, *El Caballero de Olmedo*.[1] This paucity of critical activity has been all the more mystifying when one realizes that the play stands amongst the finest pieces produced during the great age of the Spanish stage and must surely be regarded as an *acierto* of that most elusive of dramatic types —the tragedy— a form which the masters of Iberian histrionic art seem rarely to have understood. Among those who have dedicated some space to this masterwork are Marcelino Menéndez y Pelayo,[2] F. Romero y Gilsanz,[3] Fidel Fita,[4] Jean Sarrailh,[5] Inez McDonald,[6] Ramón Gómez de la Serna,[7] J. M. Blecua,[8] Enrique Anderson-Imbert,[9] Dámaso Alonso[10] Donald A.

---

[1] First published in *Veinticuatro parte perfecta de las comedias del Fénix de España* (Zaragoza, 1641).

[2] Marcelino Menéndez y Pelayo, "Observaciones preliminares," Lope de Vega, *Obras*, ed. Real Academia Española, X, lxxv-xcviii. All subsequent references to this series will be indicated RAE.

[3] F. Romero y Gilsanz, "El Caballero de Olmedo," *Revista contemporánea*, CVII, 82-102.

[4] Fidel Fita, "El Caballero de Olmedo y la Orden de Santiago," *Boletín de la Real Academia de la Historia*, XLVI, 398-422.

[5] Jean Sarrailh, *El Caballero de Olmedo*, edition and prologue (Paris, 1935).

[6] Inez MacDonald, *El Caballero de Olmedo*, edition and notes (Cambridge, England, 1935).

[7] Ramón Gómez de la Serna, "El Caballero de Olmedo," *Revista Cubana*, XIV, 38-59.

[8] J. M. Blecua, "Nota al *Caballero de Olmedo*," *Nueva revista de filología hispánica*, VIII, 190.

[9] Enrique Anderson-Imbert, "Lope dramatiza un cantar," in *Grandes libros de occidente* (Mexico, 1957), 63-74.

Yates,[11] A. A. Parker,[12] C. A. Soons,[13] and M. Bataillon.[14] Yet for all the luster of these names, curiously no one has attempted to examine the play carefully in terms of its being a tragedy and of the component literary and dramatic traditions which constitute its background. This is not to assert, by any means, that the labors of my predecessors have proved unsatisfying: indeed, the present essay must acknowledge a great debt to previous endeavor, since each of the *mélange* of scholars mentioned above has contributed a significant perspective to a better comprehension of the *Caballero*.

But the fact remains that our tragedy richly deserves a more developed body of critical writing than has hitherto been accorded to it. This may be due to the unusual complexity of the play's conception and execution. *El Caballero de Olmedo,* however disarming it may appear in its seeming simplicity, is not a piece to be regarded lightly, nor approached with anything short of a solemn seriousness. To offer less is to depreciate its marvelous unity. Nor, I hold, should the investigator make the fatal error of assuming that the *Caballero* represents but another instance in the turgid body of writings which swells the glory of the *Celestina* by way of imitation. This *caveat* may, by the way, at least partially explain why so little time has been spent on such a masterwork. Arriving at an aesthetic insight into the secrets of Rojas's *tragicomedia* does not necessarily provide a key that will open the door to the inner chamber of Lope's creativeness as expressed in this play. More will be said about this inescapable comparison in another place.

The purpose of the following study is to examine in some length and detail the tragedy as tragedy: that is, to analyze it rigorously within the assumption that the *Caballero* was addressed

---

[10] Dámaso Alonso, "Tres procesos de dramatización," in *De los siglos oscuros al de oro* (Madrid, 1958), 144-147.

[11] Donald A. Yates, "The Poetry of the Fantastic in *El Caballero de Olmedo,*" *Hispania*, XLIII, 503-507.

[12] A. A. Parker, "The Approach to the Spanish Golden Age Drama," *Tulane Drama Review*, IV, 42-59.

[13] C. Alan Soons, "Towards an Interpretation of *El Caballero de Olmedo,*" *Romanische Forschungen*, LXXIII, 160-168.

[14] Marcel Bataillon, *La Célestine selon Fernando de Rojas* (Paris, 1961), 238-250.

1. SOURCES   17

to an audience of the seventeenth century. My critical presuppositions are the following: the play is an autonomous artistic unity—not a reworking of the *Celestina;* it was fashioned from several literary and social traditions existing prior to the seventeenth century and which Lope's public shared with him as a common inheritance; and, finally, dramatic art is effective to the degree that the reality it creates is affective, i. e., projects "over" the stage and touches the spiritual and psychological antennae of the human condition which alone can impose form on experience.

A few words of orientation for the reader concerning the organization and logic of this essay are in order. We shall begin with an inquiry into the known immediate sources of the legend. Then, the literary and social traditions within which Lope interpreted his materials will be studied. Finally, an attempt to correlate this information with a structural scrutiny of the play will be made in order to demonstrate the integration of the constituent conventions and their adjustment to the demands of tragedy. I must beg my reader's indulgence if he feels at times that he is being led through a labyrinth of quotations and materials with which he is probably already familiar. The rationale in this procedure is simply to reactivate sensitivities and to condition receptivity to the tissue of the play and my study of it. If I can avoid having it said that I have stormed in where angels fear to tread I shall be satisfied.

The Immediate Sources of the Legend

Father Fidel Fita says, in his study on the Order of Santiago and the play, that one Alonso Pérez de Vivero occupied a position of no small responsibility in the Court of Juan II as the *contador mayor* and secretary to the King.[15] As such he enjoyed considerable favor with the monarch's *privado,* don Álvaro de Luna, the Constable of Castile. During the turbulent years of the mid-fifteenth century, don Alvaro's strange ascendancy over his lord occasioned no end of jealousies and rivalries. In 1453, the constable treacherously ordered the assassination of Alonso de Vivero, who

---

[15] Fidel Fita, *art. cit.,* 399.

had fought beside him in the second battle of Olmedo. The event and the existence of don Alonso would be insignificant to this study were it not for the fact that Pérez de Vivero was the great-grandfather of don Juan de Vivero who was destined to become the source of the legend of the Caballero de Olmedo. Nor is the blood relationship of don Juan to don Alonso so important to our purpose as are the times during which the latter flourished.

Ironically, Juan de Vivero met somewhat the same fate that had taken the life of his illustrious ancestor. The first historical notice of Juan's death is recorded in Alonso López de Haro's *Nobiliario genealógico de los reyes y títulos de España* (Madrid, 1622), Second Part, Book IX, Chapter VII:

> Don Juan de Vivero, caballero del hábito de Santiago, señor de Castronuevo y Alcaraz, fue muerto viniendo de Medina del Campo de unos toros, por Miguel Ruiz, vecino de Olmedo, saliéndole al encuentro, sobre diferencias que traían, por quien se dijo aquellas cantilenas que dicen: Esta noche le mataron —al caballero/ la gala de Medina—, la flor de Olmedo. (See Menéndez y Pelayo, *op. cit.*, lxxv.)

A far more complete and dramatic account of the young nobleman's untimely demise is set forth in don Antonio Prado y Sancho's *Novenario de Nuestra Señora de la Soterrana, con siete recuerdos históricos, panegíricos y morales* which is, as Menéndez y Pelayo tells us, "...una pequeña historia de la villa de Olmedo, de la cual es patrona aquella imagen." (*Op. cit.*, lxxvi.)

> D. Juan de Vivero, caballero hidalgo de la Villa de Olmedo, pidió unos galgos a D. Miguel Ruiz de la Fuente, caballero hidalgo de la misma ciudad, el cual no los quiso dar, motivando esta negativa el deseo de venganza de parte de D. Juan. Encontráronse en el campo, y D. Juan cruzó con una vara el rostro a D. Miguel, pero el ofendido caballero no tuvo valor para vengarse en aquella ocasión. Cuando su madre lo supo, cuentan que dijo: "No soy yo D.ª Beatriz de Contreras si no te vengas de D. Juan, y de no hacerlo te echaré mi maldición". En el día 2 de noviembre del año 1521 tuvo noticia de que Vivero venía de Medina; le esperó poco antes de la Senovilla, y en el sitio que desde entonces se llama la cuesta del Caballero, y al ponerse el sol, le mató traidoramente. D. Miguel se

1. SOURCES

retiró al monasterio de la Mejorada, siendo perseguido por las justicias de Valladolid, Medina y Olmedo, pues era el caballero muerto muy calificado, y de su casa descienden los Condes de Fuensaldaña. Padeció el monasterio muchos trabajos, hasta el punto que los religiosos tuvieron que llevar el Santísimo Sacramento a Olmedo. (*Idem.*)

Don Miguel eventually fled to Mexico where he entered the Dominican Order.

According to Menéndez y Pelayo, the *Novenario* was composed about the middle of the eighteenth century. Lope could not, therefore, have had access to Prado y Sancho's work. Indeed it is likely that he did not even know of the account as set forth in the *Nobiliario*. Nor would he have needed to have read of the murder in any chronicle, since the event gave rise to what must have been at least one *romance*, a *danza* known as the "Caballero," a "Baile del Caballero de Olmedo," and possibly other forms of folk expression. All that remains of the hypothetical *romance* is the refrain mentioned in the paragraph quoted above from López de Haro. The "Baile del Caballero de Olmedo" first appeared in printed form in the *Parte VII* (1617) of Lope, although there is no proof that the lyrics are by the *Fénix*. It contains the famous refrain and is curiously reminiscent of the style of earlier ballad forms. It is, of course, entirely possible that the legend, and especially the refrain, are wholly the result of Lope's genius. More probably, however, there did exist one or more *romances* during the sixteenth century. Don Emilio Cotarelo y Mori, indeed, informs us that the "Danza" was popular in the sixteenth century.[16] But whether or not this "Danza" is in reality the hypothetical *romance* cannot be ascertained. At any rate the account of Vivero's death as narrated in the *Novenario* contains some of the dramatic elements of Lope's play, especially the insult to Miguel de la Fuente, reflected in the drama's Rodrigo, the insidious assassin of the hero.

We recall that the *Novenario* is essentially a history of the town of Olmedo. To be sure, then, Prado y Sancho's short chronicle must have been drawn from the tales, lore and history of that

---

[16] Emilio Cotarelo y Mori, *Colección de entremeses*, NBAE, XVII, CCXXXV.

region. Menéndez y Pelayo maintains that it is historically accurate in all its details. (*Op. cit.*, lxxvii.) Since Lope could not have been acquainted with the *Novenario*, and since that narration contains so many striking parallels with Lope's play (except the bullfight), parallels which become major dramatic *resortes*, it seems reasonable to conclude that the hypothetical *romance*(s) also embodied a texture of incidents not unlike those presented by the *Novenario*. Nor does it seem too far-fetched to assume, therefore, that the event itself gave rise to one or more *romances*, then to a *danza* and *baile*, and subsequently inspired not only Lope's tragedy but also an earlier one by the same title written by *tres ingenios* (1606),[17] and a *romance* artístico of Francisco de Borja. Borja's poem is unusually significant. It will be reproduced and studied closely elsewhere. For present purposes, suffice it to say that its hero is called don Juan. This version introduces several important modifications which prompted don Marcelino to state: "Tiene alguna relación con la comedia de Lope pero no procede de ella." (*Op. cit.*, lxxviii.) Borja must have known of previous *romances* antedating Lope's play, to judge by the name of the hero.

It might be well to recapitulate at this juncture the foregoing discussion and to take account of the elements of the legend to which Lope fell heir. Historically it centers about a hero of high birth and considerable social stature who is murdered treacherously by another citizen of the realm. The *Nobiliario* introduces the bullfight sequence, but the *Novenario* fails to mention it. Neither of the chronicles makes any allusion to the existence of a love affair. The idea of an insult to the hero's rival is contained in the *Novenario*. In the "Baile del Caballero de Olmedo" the account is built around the bullfight episode.[18] If the lyrics to this "Baile" are by Lope they give us an early glimpse into the dramatist's first vision of his subject matter. Of interest is the name of the hero which is the same as that of the play's protagonist. Treatments such as this one must have represented the state of the legend as the dramatist knew it, assuming, of course, that the text is not

---

[17] See E. Juliá Martínez's edition of this work, *Comedia del Caballero de Olmedo* (Madrid, 1944).
[18] See the text of the "Baile" as it appears in E. Cotarelo y Mori, *Colección, op. cit.*, XVIII, 491.

Lope's work. Several new and dramatic elements have been added to the bare historical account. First of all, the hero has become a magnificent paragon of young manhood who is deeply in love with a *dama*. He is now the idol of all the town maidens, and a master of the tauromatic art. Finally, his death is due to envy rather than differences of opinion.

This, in brief, is the *matière du chevalier* as Lope must have received it or created it himself prior to the composition of his tragedy. It contains the fundamental blueprint of the drama in that a love affair has been introduced into the primitive plot articulation, and, of course, this insertion has brought with it all of the accoutrements of the inherently dramatic. A cursory reading of the play, however, reveals that the dramatist has integrated the outlines of the legend into the pattern of the *Celestina*. The result is a far more complex and complicated expression of the *caballero* theme. The fact that Lope has placed his tragedy in the reign of Juan II, rather than during the time in which it actually occurred, is due perhaps less to his ignorance of history than to the requirements of the dramatic atmosphere in which the plot develops. In this regard the time of the action may be our first insight into the artistic consciousness of this pre-eminent craftsman as he concentrated all the vast powers of his prodigious genius on an act of aesthetic intuition and creativeness.

The mystery of the direct sources may never be resolved, beyond the obvious borrowings from Rojas's immortal work. But even if scholars could find some *romance* or other lost account which would demonstrate beyond the smallest doubt that within its verses or prose lay the immediate headwaters of the tragedy, this discovery in itself would not unravel the secret of the play's magnetic charm or, one suspects, genuinely contribute to the critical perception of its form and composition. Of far greater relevance to the aims of critical analysis is the discernment and careful study of the literary conventions and social traditions within which Lope interpreted the simple outlines of the legend. The remainder of this discussion will, accordingly, investigate this problem.

* * *

What, then, are the traditional materials and beliefs within which Lope has re-created the drama of *la gala de Medina, la flor de Olmedo?* To be brief, they are the doctrine of courtly love, witchcraft, and certain notions of medieval and Renaissance medicine. The critical justification for the selection of these three areas of consideration rests on the following logic: in themselves and in their interrelatedness they answer a number of perplexing questions which the play occasions. The first of these concerns exactly why Alonso never asks for Inés's hand in marriage. As we shall see, there is absolutely no obstacle to his doing so. When he falls in love with his lady he is totally unaware of Rodrigo's intentions. Indeed, the antagonist himself does not approach don Pedro on the subject until the end of Act I. And Inés loathes the very sight of the boorish anti-hero. Why, then, did she not suggest that Alonso speak to her father before the inevitable happened? Nor can a case be put forth that Alonso is not of the proper station. This is patently not in consonance with the image of him as a near perfect *caballero* highly esteemed by no less than the King of Castile. Furthermore, in Act III, 823-a, [19] Inés decides to make a clean confession of the whole affair to her father, whereupon we learn that he is delighted with her good taste, and would have reacted favorably from the very beginning had he known the truth. The possibility of reservations on Pedro's part, therefore, is not a factor. Finally, in the agony of death, Alonso exclaims to God that marriage has always been his sole intention. Yet from the first moments of his attraction to Inés, Christian union seems to be studiously avoided.

The second perplexing question is the existence of preternatural occurrences and of well defined psychological disturbances in the character of Alonso. The hero experiences clearly recognizable moments of clairvoyance, expressed both consciously and unconsciously, the latter in the form of a horrifying nightmare. The appearance of the ghost and the *labrador*, for all their objectivity on stage, may well be understood as inner *trastornos* when examined in the light of prevailing medical theory. A third question suggests the possibility of a relationship between the first and second queries: are the protagonist's interior anxiety and malaise related in some way to the seeming dishonesty of his intentions?

---

[19] All references to the text of the play are to *Obras escogidas*, ed. Federico Carlos Sainz de Robles (Madrid, 1958), I, 793-824.

1. SOURCES

Again, in what manner shall we account for the insistent linkage of love and death in the play? And, finally, a desultory comparison of the *Celestina* with the *Caballero* reveals as many differences as similarities, especially in the figure of Fabia, and must surely urge the spectator to ponder why Lope modified his pattern so extensively and to what purpose. An examination of the above-mentioned background material will serve to answer all of these problems and begin to provide the basis for a perceptive apparatus sensitive to further questions of form and dramatic procedure. We shall begin where Lope began —with the doctrine and poetry of courtly love— since it is in the light of this convention that the tragic affair of Alonso and Inés is best illumined.

Professor Angel Valbuena Prat has pointed out that *El Caballero de Olmedo* preserves much of the lyrical aura and atmosphere of the *cancioneros*. Indeed, according to this eminent historian of Spanish letters, the period of Juan de Mena and Garcí Sánchez de Badajoz was for the *Fénix* the age of historical antiquity.[20] It is precisely to the major collections of the love lyric of this intriguing age that the modern critic must turn to comprehend the doctrine of courtly love, which is so completely and fully preserved there. Lope was not the only poet to envision the legend of the Gentleman from Olmedo within the conceptual patterns of *la courtoisie*. In 1648 there appeared the first edition of the poetic works of don Francisco de Borja, Príncipe de Esquilache, containing his rendition of the legend.[21] The text of this *romance*, which follows, leaves not the slightest margin of doubt concerning the Príncipe's interpretation. For the reader's convenience it is reproduced here in its entirety as a prelude to the discussion of courtly love.

> Enamorado en Medina
> El caballero de Olmedo,
> Galán se parte a las fiestas
> La víspera de San Pedro.
>
> No repara en su peligro,
> Porque el amante más cuerdo,

---

[20] Ángel Valbuena Prat, *Historia de la literatura española* (Barcelona, 1950), II, 357.
[21] See M. Menéndez y Pelayo, *op. cit.*, lxxx, fn. 1.

Si es valiente con amor,
es temerario con celos.

La noche le acompañaba
En tan obscuro silencio,
Que hasta las hojas y flores
Guardó en prisiones el sueño.

Un criado le acompaña,
Segundo galán del pueblo,
En sus amores testigo,
Y en su muerte compañero.

¡Qué fuera está de pensar
De su jornada de suceso;
Que son desdichas mayores
Las que no se previnieron!

Del cancionero repite,
Cantando, los tristes versos:
"Si por ti pierdo la vida,
¡Oh qué bien, señora, muero!"

Sólo en el monte escuchaba
Silbos, y vozes de lexos;
De los perros el cuidado,
De las ovejas el miedo.

Llegó primero a Medina
Que al monte dixo el lucero
Que dormir quiere la noche
Y salir el sol despierto.

Llegó apenas, cuando vino
De su dama un escudero,
A darle la bienvenida
Al desdichado mancebo,

Y a dezirle que esta noche,
Más seguro y más secreto,
Por el jardín, como suele,
Entrar podrá en su aposento.

¡Qué largo recela el día!
Y agradecido y suspenso,
Con mil anuncios se viste,
De las fiestas cuadrillero.

1. SOURCES

Quedó deshecho en pedazos
En sus manos el espejo,
Y el caballo de la entrada
Cayó de repente muerto.

Todo le anima y le enoja;
Que siempre son los agüeros
Espuelas de los amantes
Y enfados de los discretos.

¡Qué galán salió a la plaza,
Vestido de azul y negro,
Para muestra de su amor,
Para galas de su entierro!

Con las damas apacible,
Con los toros bravo y fiero,
Robó a doña Ana los ojos
Cuando llegó los del pueblo.

Todo es enojo y ofensa
A su marido y sus deudos,
A quien descubrió el criado
De aquella noche el concierto.

Acabáronse las fiestas
Aquella tarde más presto;
Que anochece más temprano
Para desdicha el tiempo.

Apenas salió vestido
De sus lumbreras el cielo,
Cuando don Juan desdichado
Acudió galán al puesto.

En él armado le espera
Con sus parientes don Diego,
Caballeros de Medina,
No en el valor caballeros.

¿Tantos aceros se juntan
Contra un amoroso yerro?
¿Tan gran valor es vengarse?
¿Matarle tan gran trofeo?

¡Qué bien se miran y escuchan
Entre el rumor y el estruendo,

De las espadas los golpes,
De las centellas el fuego!

¡Oh, qué bien riñe don Juan!
¡Oh, qué bizarro y qué diestro!
Mas son los contrarios muchos
y yace el criado muerto.

Ni vozes ni luzes sirven
A su vida de remedio,
Que entre ofensas y venganzas
Él y otros dos la perdieron.

Desde entonces le cantaron
Las zagalas al pandero,
Los mancebos por las calles,
Las damas al instrumento:

·Esta noche le mataron al caballero,
A la gala de Medina, la flor de Olmedo.
    (Menéndez y Pelayo, *op. cit.*, lxviii-lxxx.)

2. COURTLY LOVE

Francisco de Borja's version of the story of the Gentleman of Olmedo is of capital interest. In stanza six the poet remarks that the hero is singing some verses from the *cancioneros* on his way to the celebration in Medina. More arresting still is the revelation, in stanza sixteen, that the object of the hero's affection is married. Where, but in the philosophy of courtly love, could an adulterous lover become a candidate for heroism and tragic stature? The ideological mould into which Borja has poured the basic elements of the knight's tale is remarkably more explicit than Lope's treatment. Nowhere in the play is any verbal reference made to the *cancioneros*, although, to those familiar with their verse, none is necessary. Nor is the affair involving Alonso and Inés set forth in Lope's tragedy as an adulterous one. In this it must be said that Borja is bold and Lope infinitely more subtle. Menéndez y Pelayo is of the opinion that the *romance* "tiene alguna relación con la comedia, pero no procede de ella." (*Op. cit.*, lxxviii.) But even assuming — which would be somewhat daring — that Borja's principal source of information and inspiration was Lope's *Caballero de Olmedo*, then the conclusion is inescapable that his intuition perceived in the drama the fundamental configurations of a tragic complex potentially inherent in the songs of the *gay saber*. More likely is the hypothesis that both Lope and the Príncipe drank from the cup of the same muse. This would explain why Borja has caused his hero to seek the favors of a married lady. In summary, then, both poets saw in the legend suitable material for an *asunto trovadoresco*, if the hypothetical *romances* had not already depicted it as such.

The world of passion, of chaste longing, exquisite pain, and ecstatic suffering, which the *cancioneros* and the sentimental novels express with almost wearisome insistence, reflects one of the significant moments in the development of Western conciousness. The love lyrics of the fifteenth century bespeak a complex code of social and emotional attitudes which, although centuries old by Lope's day, still constituted an exciting literary convention. To understand the motivation for this fashionable outpouring of sentimentality one must first realize that despite the unvarying rhetorical formulae, a coherent and logical core of ideas and attitudes toward love, sex, and the relationships between men and women is advanced in the *cancioneros,* and this fact must be appraised both historically, in terms of its development, and empirically, in terms of what it formulates.

The doctrine of courtly love which pervades all the poetic activity of the *cancioneros,* as is well known, had its beginnings in the South of France during the twelfth century. Exactly why and how the troubadours in the court of Guillaume d'Aquitaine developed their daring new ideas is still the subject of dispute among students of this phenomenon. The reasons for the heterodoxy of the troubadours, however, must be understood, at least in part, as a conscious reaction to the convention and tradition of marriage as it had been known for centuries. In this regard courtly love represents a declination from the center of accepted practice. In short, neither the Ancients nor the Church Fathers sanctioned passionate love. [22] At the time in which the troubadours were gathering in the ducal castles of the Midi the institution of matrimony was, for the most part, a distinctly practical arrangement, not infrequently a financial or political one having nothing to do with wooing, tenderness, emotional fulfillment, or any of the other characteristics associated with marriage today. Practicality and the simple need for procreation justified the marriage contract.

---

[22] For a more detailed account of the history of marriage, love, etc., the reader is directed to the following texts: H. Blummer, *The Home Life of the Ancient Greeks* (New York, 1893); W. H. S. Jones, *Greek Morality* (London, 1906); C. E. Robinson, *Everyday Life in Ancient Greece* (Oxford, 1933); Jerome Carcopino, *Daily Life in Ancient Rome* (New Haven, 1940); Maurice Valency, *In Praise of Love* (New York, 1958); C. S. Lewis, *The Allegory of Love* (London, 1959); Morton M. Hunt, *The Natural History of Love* (New York, 1959), and Alexander J. Denomy, *The Heresy of Courtly Love* (New York, 1947).

Needless to say, the position of womankind in this axiology of the pragmatic was decidedly a subordinate one. First came the lord, or the husband, and then his wife, who tended his household, bore his children, and raised them. The troubadours, however, saw life in a different way and they introduced into this drab and prosaic system a philosophy at once romantic, forbidden, and interesting — the heresy of courtly love. It would distort the comprehension of their outlook to fancy that it was anything greater — in its beginnings — than the materialization of the simple proclivity to be different. C. S. Lewis has wisely described *la courtoisie* as a truancy. A momentary pause to explore this term will prove to be most helpful in all that is to follow.

A genuine truancy is neither revolutionary nor nihilistic; it does not attempt to proselytize, nor does it seek to replace or displace that other set of conditions in perspective to which it is truant. On the contrary, any spiritual phenomenon which falls within this category entails recognition both tacitly and implicitly of the existence of another order. In a sense, a truancy is a small but highly articulate cell embedded within the tissue of a much greater organism. It does not, therefore, behoove the parasite body to manifest any real hostility, belligerence, or violence toward its host. To do so would be to pass from truancy to delinquency and thereby run the risk of sliding into rebellion. There is a certain logic to all of this. Without the other system, there could obviously be no truancy; thus it can be said that the deviation takes cognizance of the accepted standards by ignoring them. The very presence of a Christian tradition and conventional social morality was indispensable to the development of courtly love because they provided an axis away from which a refined élite of the sophisticated could move. The "initiated" can enjoy this distinction only in so far as there is a vast body of the "uninitiated" to guarantee the proper degree of perspective. The legitimate truancy does not aspire to become autonomous or independent, as many of the heretical sects attempted to do.[23] This would involve an outright rupture with the prevailing pattern and then all the

---

[23] For an excellent account of the early heresies which seem to connect curiously in some ways to the doctrines of the troubadours see Walter Nigg, *The Heretics*, trans. Richard and Clara Winston (New York, 1962).

delights and thrills derived from being apart would necessarily harden into the defensive posture of a minority group. The relationship of courtly love and the society which produced it is perhaps best understood as a symbiosis with the health and survival of the parent absolutely necessary to the growth of the progeny. For this reason it would be grossly misleading to represent courtly love as some sort of early romantic upheaval or wholesale disavowal of its age and milieu. The attractive feature of the troubadour's world was simply its delicious divergence from the ordinary.

Commenting on the *De arte honeste amandi* of Andreas Capellanus, the 'theoritician' of courtly love, Lewis remarks:

> Yet while Andreas thus wishes to Christianize his love theory as far as possible, he has no real reconciliation. His nearest approach to one is a tentative suggestion on the lines of Pope: "Can that offend great Nature's God which Nature's self inspires?"—on which we can have no better comment than the words of the lady in the same conversation, a few lines later, *sed divinarum rerum ad praesens disputatione omissa...* 'Leaving the religious side of the question out for a moment'—and then she turns to the real point. For the truth is that the rift between the two worlds is irremediable... Once bring *that* in, as the lover argues in the same passage, and you must give up, not only loving *par amours,* but the world as well. (*Allegory,* 40-41.)

Thus, to escape "vulgar common sense and the ten commandments" — the phrase belong to Lewis — the devotees of the cult of courtesy substituted a different set of norms for those which held together the world in which everyone else lived. In effect the twelfth-century poets of Provence constructed their own psychology, sociology, morality, mystique, logic, and rhetoric. This substitution was accomplished not as an initial dialectical system, but rather as a simple accretion and refinement of their sentiments expressed over and again by generations of poets and writers who enrolled at one time or another in the legions of love. In the examination to follow, attention will be given principally to the psychology, morality, and mystique of courtly love. The logic which regulated the anatomy of *la courtoisie* will become manifest in the discussion of the aforementioned categories. I have deliberately avoided the restriction of examples to any one country or century (although the preponderance is drawn from the *cancioneros*) in the hope that the reader will gather by this *modus operandi* that from the twelfth century to the seventeenth the courtly inspiration did not radically alter its directions or its substance.[24]

If one is ever to grasp the delectation of the courtly poets in their ceaseless sighing, 'complaining,' and perpetual professions of excrutiating pain, one must first turn his attention to the high place of the gentler sex since she was the fount of all their suffering and, therefore, of their lyrics. The *midons,* or lady, was the centerpiece on the altar erected to the God of Love, a kind of combination madonna and feudal mistress to whom the lovesick male avowed absolute fealty. Such a relationship was natural enough: feudal society had long been accustomed to the allegiance of vassal to noble, even when the noble was a woman. When we consider that courtesy developed in the castles of the Provençal nobility, it comes as no surprise that this subtle substitution of medieval fealty should appropriate some formulae of contemporary protocol. That the aristocratic lady should outrank her inferiors, if for no reason other than those of station, was a condition inherent in the social architecture of the Middle Ages. But that she should be invested with the robes of supremest perfection was a daring departure from the usual state of affairs. To the troubadour the lady represented the incarnate aggregation of all imaginable virtue. She was, so to speak, a prodigious wonder of nature, no less beauteous of spirit than of 'physick.' The traditional roles of social hierarchy have become reversed, and with this turnabout a correspondingly novel shift of attitude toward the man is revealed in the process. His stature is accordingly reduced to that of an inferior being, full of imperfections and incompletion, a rough-hewn pilgrim in quest of the light.

What is outstanding in all of this is that the poet willingly accepts subordination to the opposite sex. But, of course, to do

---

[24] This does not mean to imply that the poets of subsequent times did not put the mark of their own periods on previous endeavor. For further modifications in the development of courtly love see Valency, *In Praise:* "The Sicilians," "The New Style," and "The New Life," respectively the last three chapters of his outstanding study.

otherwise would be to violate the first article of faith in the religion of love: humility. Once the lady has been envisioned as the zenith of all radiance, it becomes logically corollary that the lover's only possible stance is one of submission. After all, to the degree that she deigns to accord him the slightest attention is his existence significant and justifiable on earth. The implementation of this cardinal vow is expressed in the notion of service to her and to all circumstances attendant upon her person and well-being. Thus, in their humility and service did the poet-lovers render constant homage to the sublime excellence of their ladies. In the theology of *Frauendienst,* to receive the lady's permission to serve is comparable to the doctrine of grace, for it denotes at once the presence of sympathy and the first spiritual emanation uniting the lover with the beloved. But, to use the language of the troubadours, leave to serve is the initial *guerdon* imparted by the *midons.* Service, then, must be understood as the means whereby the lover partakes of higher beauty, and rises to a plane of refinement superior to his own. The attitude described thus far toward women, it must be admitted, is a considerable variation from the view of their station in life generally accepted in the 'outside world.' Far from Eve's lustful and simple-minded daughters, the object of courtesy's energy has become a principle in her own right. Whether the poor ladies liked it or not, they had been placed reverently atop a pedestal, and there they would remain for centuries to come in the eyes of the admirers, be they troubadours, knights, gentlemen, or New York executives. What is disturbing is that somehow, for all of their perfection, they are rarely seen in courtly poetry, especially in the fifteenth century *cancioneros,* and then only dimly or allegorically. Despite the outpourings of anguished lyric sentiment one has the distinct impression that these ethereal creatures are essentially the aesthetic and spiritual excuse for the poet to set forth his own miserable condition. They appear to be, so to speak, medieval Dulcineas, whom no one has ever met — or heard of, for that matter. But there was a rationale to this form of blurred portraiture which will be discussed elsewhere. Suffice it to say that the poetry of courtesy must — ironically — concentrate its heat on the inner emotional flux of the lover himself rather than on the woman for whom it is intended. However much the courtly bards allege their subservience to some misty *midons*, the world they create is still, fundamentally, a masculine one. What has changed is the manner in which they choose to express their virility.

Any discussion of *Frauendienst* must inevitably face the problem of marriage, since the two institutions are necessarily implicated in a philosophy of love. Marriage, or more strictly speaking, the absence of marriage, provides the investigator with the perspective which not only defines the nature of courtly love, but also the psychology which accompanies it as well. Lord Eros, from his first visitations to the castles of the Midi, revealed to his followers that true love and matrimony were mutually exclusive terms, and Andreas Capellanus, his prophet, set the deposition down once and for all in the "book of laws," the *De arte honeste amandi*.[25] In Book II, Chapter VIII, the rejection of the nuptial bond is made the first regulating principle: "Marriage is no real excuse for not loving." (ACL, 184.) The reasoning beneath this declaration is better stated in the dialogue between a "man of the higher nobility" and "a woman of the simple nobility." The man says:

> "But I am surprised that you wish to misapply the term 'love' to that marital affection which husband and wife are expected to feel for each other after marriage, since everybody knows that love can have no place between husband and wife. They may be bound to each other by a great immoderate affection, but their feeling cannot take the place of love, because it cannot fit under the true definition of love." (*ACL*, 100.)

These asseverations, and many others like them, must obviously be understood against the drab background of medieval marriage. It will be remembered that the traditional institution of matrimony was oriented toward the disposition of a patriarchal society; the wife was subordinated in all respects to her spouse. Such a condition is precisely the point of truancy in the doctrine of *la courtoisie*. The troubadours, in reversing the traditional order,

---

[25] For the convenience of the reader I have used John Jay Parry's translation of the *De arte*, entitled *The Art of Courtly Love* (New York, 1959), henceforth abbreviated *ACL*.

therefore, saw no place whatsoever in their Utopia for the marital relationship. How can a man pay tribute to a woman who by law is his ward?[26] In fifteenth-century Spain Juan Alvarez Gato explains to his *señora* the incompatibility of the nuptial bond and true love:

> "Dezís: 'Casemos los dos,
> porque deste mal no muera,'
> Señora, no plega a Dios,
> syendo mi señora vos,
> cos haga mi compañera,
> Que, pues amor verdadero
> no quiere premio ni fuerça,
> aunque me vere que muero,
> nunca querré, ni quiero
> et que por mi parte se tuerça.
> Amarnos amos a dos
> con una fe muy entera,
> queramos esto los dos:
> mas no le plega a Dios,
> syendo mi señora vos,
> cos haga mi compañera." [27]

Within the marriage contract, by definition, there can be no difficulty. The husband is free to take what he wants, and do as he pleases; indeed, such is his mandate.

The path which led to the inner garden of love had to be difficult, strewn with obstacles — a prerequisite which made the delicious fragrance of its roses all the more desirable. It was due largely to this condition that the troubadours evolved a concept of *amor purus*, a love which expressed itself in the cultivation of either an adulterous relationship or an impossible love. True love, thus, became associated with illicit love. While marriage itself

---

[26] Service rendered by a husband to his wife, says Gui d'Ussel to his cousin, is absurd. See J. Audiau, *Les quatres troubadours d'Ussel* (Paris, 1922), 69.

[27] In *Cancionero castellano del siglo XV*, ed. R. Foulché-Delbosc, NBAE [Vols. XIX, XXII], I, 229—hereafter *CC*. I have drawn freely from the following *cancioneros*: Hernando del Castillo, *Cancionero general*, Bibliófilos Españoles, XXI [2 vols.]—hereafter *CG*; *Cancionero de palacio*, ed. Francisca Vendrell de Millás (Barcelona, 1945)—hereafter *CP*; *Cancionero gallego-castelhano*, ed. Henry R. Lang (New York, 1902)—hereafter *CGC*; and *Cancionero de Roma*, ed. M. Canal Gómez (Florence, 1935)—hereafter *CR*.

was not predicated on any assumption of erotic desire, it was no barrier to 'true love.' This is what Andreas means when he affirms that true lovers should not regard matrimony as an excuse for not loving. What was missing in the marriage contract had to be found outside of the household. The paradoxical dimension of this philosophy of obstruction is that marriage which contains no amorous sympathy becomes the bridge to what Spitzer has aptly called *le chaste eloignement*.[28] The illicit character of *amor purus* cannot be appraised as an aesthetic immorality. The very mention of the term 'immorality' gainsays a comparison with Christian convention. Courtesy has a morality of its own, as Alexander Denomy has noted:

> It is neither Christian *caritas* nor Platonic love; it is neither mystical love nor lust, but a special type of love peculiar to the troubadours. It is a love divorced from physical possession, based on the desire for it, practiced by people of worth and regarded as productive of every virtue and every good. (*The Heresy*, 25-26.)

The love of which the troubadours sang, then, must be located somewhere on the emotional spectrum between pure lust and Christian *agape*, and that point at which desire passes away from the white heat of animal possession to the intense radiance of spiritual desire is called passion.

The peculiar type of emotionality which is suffused throughout all expression of courtly love derives its force from the unique narcotic of passion. The spell in which the courteous move — if it is anything tangible — is freely admitted to be a kind of bittersweet intoxicant arising from the deadly combination of desire, physical absence, and an almost ferocious constancy. Both the followers of Eros and his detractors agree that this genus of love — passionate love — represents first and foremost a psychology of feeling. In this they oppose it to cool but dull reason. Tapia tells us that love is an ethereal and fleeting vision, an attraction born of desire, easily withered, difficult to obtain: "Es amor una

---

[28] Leo Spitzer, *L'amour lointain de Jaufré Rudel et la poésie des troubadours*, University of North Carolina Studies in the Romance Languages and Literatures (Chapel Hill, 1944), 1-2.

visión / que quan presto se figura, / tan presto desaparesce; / afición y no razón." (*CC*, II, 442.) Gonzalo de Carrillo is even more emphatic about the antagonism of love to reason: "El amor lo que procura / contradize la razón, / y lo que el seso assegura / no lo consiente passión." (*CG*, II 389.) To the courteous, from the times of Guillaume through the seventeenth century, the logic of the heart was not only preferable to reason but in its own way more convincing, and certainly more overpowering. But it was precisely this abandonment of reason, perhaps more than any other facet of their philosophy, which incurred the perpetual official enmity of the society in which they flourished. For example, Juan Luis Vives, although writing at a later date, still sees in passionate love a form of degeneracy, a madness which disturbs the higher faculties:

> El amor de la belleza es un olvido de la razón, muy cercano de la locura, vicio feo y poco conveniente al alma sana: turba el consejo, quebranta el alto y generoso espíritu y de los grandes pensamientos le derriba a los más rastreros y ruines; hácelos quejumbrosos, irascibles, temerarios, imperiosos con dureza, serviles con blandura, inútiles para todo y, al fin, hasta para el mismo amor. Pues como sea que arda en insaciable deseo de gozar, gasta mucho tiempo en sospechas, en lágrimas, en quejas; concítase el odio de todo el mundo y él mismo acaba por odiarse a sí mismo.[29]

This contrast in perspective concerning the effects of passionate love is central to the understanding of the courtly phenomenon through the seventeenth century. The conflict, here expressed as the view of an 'insider' looking out, as opposed to that of an 'outsider' peering in, is manifest in the literature of the Renaissance throughout and lends itself especially well to the dramatic art.

Since the courtly lover preferred that his ladies be kept at a distance, it followed that his passion became all the more ardent precisely because there was no hope of erotic fulfillment. In fact, pure love by definition did not admit satisfaction. Paradoxically, *amor purus* was a love supported on chastity. The troubadours

---

[29] Juan Luis Vives, *Obras completas*, ed. Lorenzo Riber (Madrid, 1947), I, 1050.

reasoned that once passion was fulfilled then it lost some of its enrapturing force, and even ran the risk of inviting its own death. Thus, Juan de Torres cautions his heart that it should not seek to avoid *cuydado:* "Ya sabes que tu cuydado, / non se puede feneçer / nin tu pesar en plazer / nunca puede ser tornado..." (*CP,* 288). What the poets of *la cortesía* sought was a form of inner tension which sprang endlessly from a tautness of the concupiscible appetite. Desire was the mainspring of this mechanism. Attraction toward the lady begat desire, and desire, in its turn, depended on longing. In this emotional circle the flame of love grew ever more ardent and created a self-renewing spiritual combustion. The concept of courteous love, therefore, rests on philosophical, psychological and medical assumptions. Courtly passion, moreover, waxes stronger in proportion to the size and number of obstacles placed in the lover's path. Love is essentially an emotional continuum which is passionate in its constitution: thus those factors which strengthen the continuum become integral to its very preservation. Now, *amor purus* implies chastity, and this vow is the chief obstacle which renews desire and maintains tension. The love of another's wife brings with it a set of conditions which function in much the same way. To begin with, the courteous lover would bring dishonor and shame on his lady were he to reveal her identity. Thus he must confine his passion to a secret relationship and content himself with furtive glances, distant contemplation, and prolonged absence from the beloved. Hernando de Ludueña, emphasizing the categorical need for secrecy, affirms that the *galán* can lose everything if he lacks *discreción:* "...mas todo le faltara / si le falta discreción." (*CC,* II, 719-a.)[30] The greater the obstacle the greater the difficulty, and we recall that Andreas accords to difficulty the fourteenth place in his catalogue of rules: "The easy attainment of love makes it of little value: difficulty of attainment makes it prized." (*ACL,* 185.) Montoro confesses he has lost his heart in a place which is unthinkable to visit: "Mi coraçon se fue perder / amando a quien no pudo haver. / Si lo perdi por mal buscar / ¿do lo ire fallar?" (*CP,* 130.) The *amor deshonesto* thus serves to interpose distance between the lovers, and this absence which results

---

[30] Cf. Suero de Ribera: "...mas de mi no saberan/ por quien digo este refrán," in *CP,* 172.

from distance is highly desirable because it makes the heart grow fonder as Juan de Torres proclaims: "Una hora que no vea / senyora, vuestra figura, / mi coraçon vos dessea / e sempre iamas se cura." (*CP*, 288.) [31] Since distance, absence, and secrecy are the waters which nourish the flower, what can be more logical than that the *midons* should be unavailable, that is, belong by law to someone else?

If the religion of love sets a premium on passion, then it follows that the greatest good is the privilege of courtship. Capellanus would allow a minimum of bodily contact, but it must never go beyond simple tactile communication. (*ACL*, 122.) The same sexology of joyous frustration is pronounced by Bartolomé de Torres Naharro, who further adds that it is enough to have desired the ultimate joy: "No biuo desesperado, / si bien dexo de os gozar; / que un bien de bienes sin par / basta hauerlo desseado." [32] And Quevedo declares at a later date that the practitioners of pure love would be suspect of transgression were they to hope for more than the right to bask in the pure warmth of passion's flame: "El amor, en brazos corre de la esperanza, porque desea unirse con lo que ama, y aquel esperar es amor. Sospechoso es el amor que espera alcanzar algo de quien ama." [33]

One should not suppose that this doctrine of continual longing, flaming desire, and self-imposed frustration conceals a latent masochism with no spiritual dimension to regulate it. The end of love's labors lifted man to a superior level of inner nobility and hence transmuted his base substance to a finer essence. It is only just, therefore, to outline this mystique of courtly love. The objection to marriage inherent in the philosophy of courtly love is that this institution is regarded as an arrangement of social and sexual convenience. It could not, by its very complexion, offer to either the husband or the wife an experience which might reshape and beautify their souls. How could such a contract provide the basis

---

[31] Cf. Suero de Ribera: "Senyora, maguer absente,/ siempre vos tengo presente," in *CP* 172.

[32] "Romance II," in *'Propalladia' and Other Works*, ed. Joseph E. Gillet (Bryn Mawr, 1943), I, 223.

[33] Francisco de Quevedo, "Sentencia 1075" in *Obras completas en prosa*, ed. Luis Astrana Marín (Madrid, 1932), 834.

for self-completion when its only purpose was to fulfill racial obligations and implement the demands of social cohesion? The troubadours wanted something more rewarding from the relationship between men and women than cold practicality. Courtly love developed — at least partially — as a means to satisfy this impulse without having to renounce the world. Behind the doctrine of love stands a theory of perfection and transfiguration of the spirit. Frederick Locke has pointed out that this vision represents a unique event in the history of love:

> The poetry of the troubadours and that of the *trouvères* in the North of France speaks of a love which, while essentially adulterous, inspires the man with nobility of character and offers him, through the beloved, a transcendent experience. It is this power of transformation which, more than anything else, constitutes the distinguishing characteristic of courtly love, a love which both as a literary theme and as a social idea is something entirely new on the European scene, and from which our modern notions of romantic love derive in a large measure. Without courtly love, the passionate love of the modern novel and theater would be difficult to explain.[34]

When Andreas tells us that "love causes a rough and uncouth man to be distinguished for his handsomeness" (*ACL*, 31), and that pure love "is distinguished by being of such virtue that from it arises all excellence of character" (122), he has already made some assumptions which seem to him to be so self-evident that he does not bother to take the time to set them forth. The first is that love's potential to improve the spirit is a magic available to Everyman, although, perhaps, it is more efficacious amongst the nobility. More important, however, is the tacit admission that man — that is, the male sex — is imperfect. Any theory of transcendency constructs its *via iluminativa* on the notion that man's constitution is base, an inferior substance in an order of nature which ascends upward to superior categories of being.[35] As a logical correlative

---

[34] See his "Introduction" to Andreas Capellanus, *The Art of Courtly Love,* translated by John Jay Parry and abridged by Frederick W. Locke (New York, 1957), vi.

[35] For a most illuminating discussion of the ascending order of nature see Otis H. Green, *Spain and the Western Tradition* (Madison, 1964), II, 3-30.

to this presupposition it is understood that what is corruptible, and perhaps corrupted, is also perfectible. In this, transcendentalism betrays a philosophical or theological optimism whenever and wherever it occurs. The reward for those who would submit themselves conscientiously to the system is progressive refinement and ultimate — if theoretical — purification which brings with it a greater nobility of character, increased self-awareness, beatitude: in short, all the promises of completion which the *askesis* holds forth. The final *guerdon* with which courtly love lured its converts was courtesy, a condition of the soul and a state of mind which was supposed to add a vastly positive dimension to the measure of man. But courtesy betrays the uncomplimentary image of man from which the troubadours departed in all of their thinking. Through love, courtesy was acquired, the spirit ennobled, base nature purified, and the lover emerged transfigured by the light of his own virtue. Valency likens true love to a school in which the lover achieves perfection. (*In Praise*, 178.) This is why the Chaplain remarks: "All courtesy comes from the plentiful stream of love..." (*ACL*, 58.) The lowly conception of man also explains why the courtly poet projected upon his lady the light of absolute ideality and swore eternal vassalage to her. The oath represented an admission of inferiority and hence called for a vow of humility. And she, high up on her pedestal, was the beacon which guided "the transport of the soul upwards to ultimate union with light, something far beyond any love attainable in this life," in the words of De Rougement.[36]

If self-transcendence was love's secret purpose, the way to the top of the summit was torturous. Catharsis implies purification, and purification in turn has always demanded sacrifice and suffering as the condition *sine qua non* of worthiness. The aspiring lover, like the mystics who borrowed so much of courtesy's rhetoric, could never be sure whether his passion would transmute the bleeding heart into a fountain of radiance or would cast it sear and rent into a hell of agonizing despair. Such was the risk — rather, the gamble — which the true lover assumed. More often than not love's initiates poured forth a steady stream of highly

---

[36] Denis De Rougemont, *Love in the Western World* (New York), 1957, 68.

charged emotional description dedicated to the memory of their pain and inability to reach the uppermost pinnacle. Macías laments that the greater his desire for inner nobility the greater was his fall into abandonment: "Cuidei sobir en alteza / por cobrar mayor estado, / e cai en tal pobreza / que moiro desamparado." (*CGC*, 7.) The manner in which Macías has expressed his disillusionment is worthy of some attention, partly because it provides insight into the nature of the courtly *askesis,* and partly because it will become central to later discussion. The rhetorical device which the poet has chosen was a favorite one amongst all the songsters of the *gay saber*. It can best be described as a kind of paradox which, in retrospect, is seen by the poet as an irony. Thus the immediate cause of the poet's inspiration is his present state of woe resulting from having aspired to inaccessible bliss. In the assault on the mountain, Macías has fallen into the pit: the greater the aspiration, the more calamitous the disappointment. The extent of happiness becomes directly proportional to the obverse of happiness in most cases. In Diego de San Pedro's *Cárcel de amor* we read: "La llaga es muy grande mas es tan ufana / que quanto es más pena mi gloria es mayor"; or "...tan grande es el bien quan grande es el mal, / porque ésta es la ley perfecta de amor." [37] Juan del Encina's *quanto más... tanto más* is the instrument most often heard: "...quanto más pena nos dieren [las damas], / quanto más mal nos hizieren, / tanto más bien les hagamos." (*CG*, II, 375.)

The paradoxical equation is the most suitable device for expressing the peculiar constitution of the catharsis which love imposed upon the devout. When its frequent use is related to the canons of courtly dogma, that is, when form and substance are compared, a clearer pattern of the mystique of passion begins to emerge. Thus, if we accomodate the way in which we examine the logic of *la cortesía* to the design of this formula, we find that courtly protocol creates an internal unity of thought which is delicately, if not precariously, balanced on a circular rather than a syllogistic logic. Unlike the format of a syllogism which deduces identities from general premises and specific cases, the *modus operandi* of passion establishes a chain of equivalences through a

---

[37] M. Menéndez y Pelayo, *Orígenes de la novela*, NBAE, VII, 73.

system of reasoning which links associated ideas. The result is that the traditional conclusion becomes a paradoxical implication of profound significance for true lovers.

The lines by Macías quoted above are representative of love's fundamental assumptions: in the contemplation of and service to 'milady's' perfection lies the road to transfiguration or courtesy. Love, then, is implicated in the urge to attain excellence. The first series of equivalences, therefore, is: perfection begets attraction, which is love. With the coming of love, desire is born. Once *deseo* has been ignited, the process of progressive refinement which leads to courtesy has begun. Thus, to love is to desire, which is to purify. But, as we have seen, if desire is to wax ever more intense, it should not ever be satisfied lest the flame which dissolves all impurities be snuffed out prematurely. It is far more convenient for this reason that the lady be married. Characteristically, then, love is synonymous with desire, and desire, because of the presence of an impediment, remains forever unsatisfied. Unrequited desire, under these conditions, changes to a longing which becomes all the more piercing because the lover should not be physically near the lady. From this disposition of relationships emerges a second series of equivalences which is paradoxical also: the longing to be with is a function of distance and absence. Since refinement is the by-product of longing, separation, therefore, is the means by which the lover draws closer to his beloved in perfection or courtesy.

Accustomed as modern man is to believing that healthy love depends on a logical resolution of the erotic impulse and that love is known by the blissful feeling of happiness which accompanies it, it will seem strange indeed —perhaps even perverse— to discover that the medieval poets of love take delight in describing, not their ecstasy, but rather their agony. The *cancioneros* constitute a hymn of praise to excruciating pain. The song of love played on the fifteenth-century *vihuela amorosa* sounds more like the lament of a lonely nightingale than a joyous melody entoned to emotional bliss. This typical emphasis on suffering is but another phase in the circular logic of courtly love. If longing is the fuel of purification, it is also the source of intense pain. From the necessary separation of the lovers arises the agony of courtly *askesis*. Pedro de Santa Fe would go even further and seek out suffering: "En tal punto m'a llegado / amor después que te veo / que deseo haver deseo / e lazro por ser lazrado." (*CP*, 203.) The Arçydiano de Toro informs his reader that the day he fell in love all happiness was lost. (*CGC*, 17.) And Iñigo López de Mendoza regards pain as the attendant circumstance of hope. (*CGC*, 97.) Illustrations of the desirability of suffering could be multiplied *ad infinitum*. What is of importance here is that the *trabaxo amoroso* is a spiritual commitment of courtly love, and that the value or virtue of the ultimate *galardón* is proportional to the degree of torment experienced by the poet. Refinement or happiness, therefore, has become a consequence of pain and suffering. This leads to the second paradox of courtesy's mystique: the joy of love, which alone can catapult man into self-transcendence, logically implies a rigid catharsis of pain through which the courtly aspirant must travel on his way to the garden of perfection. The equivalence of 'happiness — pain' is a corollary of this paradox. It now should be perfectly understandable why the *cancionero* poets dwell so insistently upon themselves and the delicious torments which they never tire of savoring: the presence of suffering indicates the reality of true love, and thus the steady growth of inner nobility and higher virtue can be physically measured. Juan Agraz makes this categorically clear: "con tanta pena / creçio mi alegria..." (*CP*, 279.)

The mystique of love, with all its equivalences and paradoxical conclusion-implications, can now be reduced to its fundamental logic. The basic links which constitute the premises are: refinement (courtesy), longing (desire), separation (adulterous or impossible love, distance), and suffering. Each of these quantities, while separable for the purposes of analysis, is adjusted to another, thereby forming a unity of doctrine. The nature of the relationships between links defines the peculiar circular cohesion so characteristic of courtly emotion and protocol. At the top of the circle, so to speak, is courtesy, which is the function of longing. Separation is a necessary cause of longing. Suffering is the result of distance and separation and, therefore, is related to longing in that both considerations arise from an obstacle. To complete the cycle, suffering is in turn an *a-priori* condition of purification and virtue. The following figure will make this spiritual movement more precise:

```
          Courtesy (Refinement, virtue)
         /        \
  Suffering        Longing (Desire)
         \        /
          Separation (Obstacle, distance)
```

Such is the underlying conceptual framework on which the Temple of Love was erected. There is, however, a dark side to this delightful edifice. Passion and death are so frequently mentioned in the same breath that Denis De Rougemont has posited in his book, *Love in the Western World,* the existence of an unconscious subterranean identity of the two states. His central thesis is that passion expresses an elaborately disguised (and therefore consciously unrecognized) yearning for death which, he declares, is the secret of the Western psyche. Passion for De Rougemont is *Liebestod,* the self-annihilating factor which seeks final repose in death's embrace. Speculation on absolute meaningfulness is always exciting, for who would not like "to draw the veil of maya" aside and catch a glimpse, however fleeting, of changeless, timeless reality? De Rougemont invites us to peer into the somber beyond with him through the medium of courtly poetry on the assumption that expression and communication are identical. It would seem that the weakness of the Swiss scholar's reasoning is that he has not taken into account the mechanism of metaphor. It is one thing to affirm objectively a desire to die: it is quite another to describe the painful reality *as if* it were death; and still another to resolve the emotional tensions of a complicated narrative in death. The first is a statement of fact; the second a rhetorical convention; the third a conclusion made unavoidable by the disposition of its own logic. Against any assumption that human articulation "secretly" reflects hidden presentiments of metaphysical and psychological absolutes it must be insisted that language — especially poetic language — is an arbitrary and imperfect system of semaphores, a fragile instrument that at best can provide its user with insights, approximations, subjective analogies, but cannot be made consubstantial with reality. The word is the handle by which we hope to seize truth: it is not the truth itself.

Although *Love in the Western World* cannot be accepted as the revelation of a latter-day gnostic, it does have a value which is not inconsiderable by any means in that its author calls attention to the extraordinary frequency with which the courtly muse implicates love in death. It is a problem which cannot and should not be avoided. Consonant with the paradoxical character of courtly passion, he who would participate in the rituals of Lord Eros soon finds that to love — the *maximum bonum* — is to experience the agony of death. Montoro reconstructs this seeming contradiction for us:

> Por se perder cuytas le dan
> et puso a mi en tal afan
> que bivo asi
> sin le cobrar
> por le contentar.
> Alli do piensa bevir
> ffaze a mi solo morir
> mas, pues alli piensas durar
> devolo desear. (*CP*, 130.)

Macias, too, realizes that if the radiant heart seeks warmth in love's flame it must be prepared for final extinction on the altar of passion: "Pero mais non averei / se non ver e desejar, / e por én assi direi: / Quen en carcer sol viver, / en carcer deseja morrer." (*CGC*, 8.) From anguished lines similar to these, De Rougemont has derived his hypothesis. Indeed, it would seem that the courtly poets do appear to yearn for death and the solace of final oblivion. Their preoccupation with the cessation of life has prompted D'Arcy to remark:

> Love is a rapture, a divine transport; it desires union with the infinite, and from that union there is no return. This means that it is a form of death, a night into which we must pass. Night, therefore, and darkness always figure in this love when it is described.[38]

The somber shadows which pervade so much of this poetry dedicated to the exaltation of amatory ecstasy are generated from two sources: the chain of equivalent implications inherent in the circular logic of the courtly mystique, and the corpus of rethorical

---

[38] Martin D'Arcy, *The Mind and Heart of Love, Lion and Unicorn: A Study of Eros and Agape* (London, 1945), 202.

conventions which the troubadours and their disciples evolved to express their doctrine.

It was demonstrated above that courtesy is related to longing, separation, and suffering. It is in the implications which the last two factors embody that the key to the peculiar life-death and living-dying formula lies. Distance and separation are guaranteed by the impossible attraction. The greater the wall separating the lover from his lady, the more intense is the effect of absence from her, and thus suffering becomes proportionately more acute, thereby yielding purest courtesy. What better way can be imagined to describe the soul-searing pain of passion than to liken it to death's cold kiss? Rhetorically, at least, the lacerating torment germane to the courtly catharsis finds its most adequate comparison in death's throes. Now the logic of *la courtoisie* has a strange proclivity for working its way out to the final implications. When we consider that absence from the lady is the source of energy upon which longing and suffering feed, then it follows that the separation which has no limit —death itself— assures perpetual absence and infinite distance. If self-fulfillment, the life abundant, is passion's supreme harmonic, that which prolongs the sweet torment, draws it out into the timeless dimension of the eternal — death — must be the chord which vibrates in sympathy with love's power to transfigure its devotees. This is why Macías feels the inner accomodation of desire, life, and death to be so meaningful. To seek the full life in love, García de Medina tells us, is to discover that desire is the antechamber to the eternal:

> Coraçon, morir, morir,
> triste, rico de deseo,
> cativo, pobre; menguado
> de cuantos bienes yo veo,
> di, maldito, sin mentir
> di tu muerte t'as buscado... (*CP*, 272.)

Death, therefore, within the design of courtly logic, is both the final obstacle and the transit to supremest virtue. In the *Cancionero de Roma* there is a lengthy composition by Lope de Estúñiga which is unusually apropos to this discussion. (*CR*, I, 4.) When passion becomes endless it also achieves immortality, transcending this life and living on after death. Estúñiga's poem

2. COURTLY LOVE

purports to be the anguished cries of a departed lover's soul reverberating across eternity and piercing the very barrier which separates the finite from the infinite. In a torrential flow of emotionality — *llorat, la triste passion, gemidos, gemid, sospirar, padescer, perescer, quebrantarse, partirse, desastrado* — the wailing poet lays bare the ardor of what must have been a passion like unto none other, and which eventually consumed him in its heat. Since death has parted the two lovers there can be no hope of union, or even reunion, and thus the poet will forever suffer and despair. The complaints and invectives he hurls from his vaporous residence serve only to remind us of the magnitude of his passion, for death's kiss has eternalized this love. Estúñiga's lament amply demonstrates the radius of implication which the chain of poetic equivalences could circumscribe. Pure love is phoenix-like in its power of self-renewal. Thus as the lover transcends himself he approaches rebirth into the new life of lasting virtue. Eternal love, then, is life everlasting achieved through insurmountable separation, suffering without respite; a state of being unfettered by earthly limitations of time and space. The ultimate event, transfiguration, is attained in the only condition capable of resolving all of these prerequisites: death.

Thus courtly logic arrives at its conclusions by a circular logic that links synonymous terms. Each section of the chain is joined to the following one by semantic implication rather than by deduction. This mode of procedure has several peculiar characteristics. First of all, a paradox will eventually be formed, hence the typical irrationality of courtly love. Circular thinking is essentially 'arational.' Second, it conjoins its premises by associating mutually common intellectual denominators. For example: life is passion; passion demands an obstacle; obstacles imply separation and distance and also create suffering; death guarantees separation and distance and prolongs pain, etc., etc. Separation and death are tangential concepts in that both participate in a common association: absence. When we become aware that circular logic carries us from one inescapable inevitability to another, it is possible to understand that the preoccupation with death in the courtly mystique is really nothing more than the final segment of association which completes the meandering circle and thus links the end to the beginning. The aesthetic cause of courtly rhetoric, together with the elaborate allegorical forms it generated, becomes, in the light of this discussion, a case of *res ipsa loquatur*. The arsenal of figures, tropes, metaphors, and similes represent poetic translations of segments of courtesy's wheel of associations. In any investigation of courtly love, logic and rhetoric are, in the last analysis, inextricable quantities. Death, therefore, must be envisioned as both a rhetorical metaphor and an inexorable conclusion-implication of the *gay saber*.

Returning momentarily to Estúñiga's creation mentioned above, it can now be seen that the architecture of its conception, as well as the patterns of diction with which he has adjusted his vision to poetry, have taken on a new richness. As stated previously, the poem purports to be the utterances of the lover's shade. Thus we are given the impression that the course of his life spent in devotion to the lady (who is not named) was at least as painful as the remembrance of it in the after life. Even in death the torment of this love will not cease: "...llorad la triste passion / de mi, muerto et non finado." (*CR*, I, 4.) And again a few lines farther along: "...llorad por tal que mi muerte / non puede matar mi daño." (*CR*, I, 4.) Passion has survived the demise of the body; it has been immortalized. What is especially peculiar about this poem is that it is *a plancto* that falls midway between a palinode and a *caveat*. The poet does not go so far as to recant his foolishness. Yet the entire composition appears to warn whoever the object of all the imperatives is that love can lead only to unutterable distress and death. Paradoxically, then, the catalogue of complaints and miseries, the *plancto* dedicated to himself, does, in effect, constitute a strange kind of funeral hymn in praise of love, since nowhere does the deceased lover even hint that in return for physical being and health he would gladly abjure his vows to the god of love. In death as in life he seems to derive a unique delight compounded of woe and ecstasy from reviewing the symptomatology of passion's syndrome. While he himself is unwilling to condemn love, he does warn the reader to flee the dangerous narcotic. Interestingly, among the metaphors Estúñiga chooses to express this admonition is the following: "...gemid la triste cadena, / cadena que me prendió." (*CR*, I, 4.) For, once the victim has become ensnared by the first of love's precepts, all the other links in the chain will indeed twine around the aching heart causing it to beat more quickly. In substance, don Lope warns that passion is like an opiate which, if consumed, creates a thirst that can never be slaked, albeit the appetite for it provides uncommon pleasure. From Estúñiga's extension of passion's force beyond death to the transfiguration of the lover in death as it occurs in Renaissance high tragedy is only the difference between sympathetic compassion and empathic participation. One can do little more than commiserate with the ailing victim of the *plancto:* but tragedy —if it is tragedy— demands quite another response. In summary, then, courtly logic, mystique, and rhetoric enriched by the subtleties of Neo-Platonic dialectic and, perhaps, even the work of the mystics, cleared the path for the positive reception of love as legitimate material for the tragic art.

This examination of the mechanism and characteristics of the courtly phenomenon would be incomplete without a final word concerning orthodox reaction to it. As Alexander Denomy has pointed out, the sweet songs of the Midi clashed with the doctrines of the Church Fathers. (*The Heresy*, 38-39.) Even Andreas is very much aware of the inherent conflict between love's practice and service to God. The Chaplain does, however, attempt to justify Eros: "I belive that God cannot be seriously offended by love, for what is done under the compulsion of nature can be made clean by an easy expiation." (*ACL*, 111.) For all of his apparent seriousness, nevertheless, Andreas fully realized that the philosophy of nature and 'reason' which he so boldly sets forth in the *De amore*, after all had been said, was a delightful but potentially very dangerous game. It is not surprising, then, that having completed the treatise, he wrote another from an entirely Christian point of view in which all of his previous advice and rules are roundly condemned. The *De reprobatione* vigorously defends Christian morality. Here he reminds his readers that sound theology insists on the antagonism between the flesh and God's grace. "What Andreas teaches to be true according to nature and reason," Denomy writes, "he teaches to be false according to grace and divine authority. Thus emerges in his work the docrine of the so-called 'double truth'." (*The Heresy*, 39.)

With the *De reprobatione* the pattern for all subsequent courtly activity was set. Sooner or later the time would come when the joy of having participated, however sincerely, in this forbidden pastime would weigh heavily on the consciences of generations of poets. Secret courtships, illicit loves, the voluntary submission to a continuum of pain and suffering, all of the apparatus and legislation pertinent to courtesy may have produced the illusion of an inner spiritual nobility, but the fact remained that somehow it was not conducive to making peace with God the Maker. The courtly gesture eventually gave way to repentance and at times to bitter disavowal which took the form of a characteristic palinode. After the game had exhausted its attractiveness the truant children who had played at it with such ardor returned quietly to the house from which they had escaped temporarily, there to recant their disobedience, attend to their wounds, and seek forgiveness. At the time of his death *(fynamiento)* the Arcidiano de Toro wrote:

> A Deus, Amor, A Deus, el Rei,
> que eu ben serví;
> a Deus, la Reinna a quen loei
> e obedecí.
> A Deus, mundo enganador,
> que eu ja me vou
> para Deus, nosso Sennor,
> que me chamou;
> e ir-me-ei u m'em mandou
> sen mais tardar,
> que non me conven morar
> ja mais en ti. (*CGC*, 20-21.)

The homecoming was probably as sincere as the leavetaking; to be sure, the old familiar scenery was safer, if less exciting. In the end, the bosom of the Church usually proved to be more accessible than that of the distant *midons*.

3. ALCAHUETERÍA AND BRUJERÍA

The anatomy of tragedy is predicated on an ontological dualism expressed in various styles as an irony. The peculiar achievement of the tragic disposition of events presents the spectator a metaphysical reconciliation of human autonomy with the grand design of nature. On the one hand man is imaged as embodying a significance which is purposeful to the order of the universe. In man the creative principle has fashioned an eye, an organ of vision and perception, through which nature is contemplated, measured, and described, and the very order in which man exists is made recognizable, available, to a mind other than that of the prime mover. If nature has eternally flattered man by placing him at the summit of her scale of perfection, she has also laid upon him —as payment for this honor— the crushing responsibility of understanding the pattern of the universe, and thus of locating the place and function of all creatures in it. Through man, creation is revealed: his purpose, therefore, is that of an historian, eternally dissecting, plotting, assembling the segments of his own perception and affirming the existence of unity. As recorder, he occupies a central locus and thus enjoys a kind of independent preeminence by virtue of his mission. As chronicler, his office is precarious in that he must at once participate in, yet be independent of, the forces of generation and the laws of regulation which govern the whole cosmos. The theory of macrocosmos and microcosmos, itself an achievement of revelation through man's intelligence, attests to the characteristic subordinate independence which nature has bestowed on her most perfect terrestrial offspring.

The dualism which lies quietly beneath the configuration of tragedy reflects this condition of dependent autonomy vouchsafed to *homo sapiens*. It is the luminosity which is suffused through the tragic articulation of events and finally, through catastrophe, enlightens the spectator by reminding him that man, for all of his unique privileges, is himself a part of a much greater design. His independence turns out to be only relative, not absolute. The nerve center of tragedy is thus implicated in the problem of accomodating individual fate to universal destiny. Tragedy seeks ultimately to purge from the spectator's purview any notion that the man-universe dualism is an antagonism or even a polarity. Thus the drama it sets forth is not so much that of the conflict between good and evil, as that of the incapacity of man to comprehend in life the delicate balance of force and counter-force, creation, and extinction, the finite and the infinite which constitute the connective tissue of the universal order. What occurs in tragedy is what must occur. It is neither good nor bad: we leave the amphitheater wiser and more comforted than when we arrived, neither in tears nor in joy, but rather in solemn reconciliation. Tragedy provides a window through which the spectator witnesses the enactment of nature's *apologia* for the mystery of life and death, the enigma of generation and decease.

In the tension of force and counter-force, tragic drama is engendered. In balance with the positive innocence of young love, albeit misguided, is the dark and shadowy world of which Fabia is the focal point. If the portrait of youthful exuberance and foollishness in this play is painted with the bright pigments of courtly love, its counter-reality —*alcahuetería* and sorcery— represents the negative condition of nature in which the lovers' passion is implicated. Forbidden love and forbidden knowledge are the diastole and systole of Lope's tragedy, the mutual correlatives of which the tragic irony is compounded. The examination of witchcraft which follows, therefore, is warrantable on several counts. The presence of Fabia relates the action —secret passion— to the counteraction—the disposition of forces in nature which conspire to bring about the catastrophe. When we pause to consider that this love affair might have been sustained without Fabia, that Alonso's premature death could have been set forth as the exclusive consequence of Rodrigo's jealousy without any reference made to Fabia, then it should become clear that in Lope's design Fabia's image is integral to the anatomy of the tragedy. The goetic alter-surface of her character is revealed time and again in her own actions and remarks, and through Rodrigo's expostulation at a crucial moment in Act III; it is powerfully suggested in the series of eery supernatural occurrences in the final Act and in the clairvoyant moment which the hero experiences. Indeed, the somber shadow which Fabia casts over all the play's action was surely what Lope intended to create. The carefully orchestrated texture of clues enumerated above was set forth to indicate to the spectator that Fabia was essentially far more than a mere latter-day daughter of Celestina. When the witchcraft phenomenon is examined, felt, as it were, through the apparatus of a seventeenth-century receptivity, the dramatic delineation of Fabia acquires a conditioning perspective which a modern reader, as steeped in his 'rational superstitions' as Lope's audiences were in their folk beliefs, might well overlook. Through Fabia Lope activates the Medieval-Renaissance terror of the black arts, the occult sciences, and thus calls forth in his *mosqueteros* all the associations popularly surrounding the witch.

Before exploring this field of sensitivity common to Lope's times, a *caveat* is necessary. The striking resemblance between *El Caballero de Olmedo* and its obvious model, the *Celestina*, makes a comparison of Fabia with the fifteenth-century bawd unavoidable. The similarity of the two *alcahuetas*, as well as the masterworks in which they appear, is more than offset by the differences separating them. In Act I of Rojas's *tragicomedia*, during the course of Párrmeno's conversation with his master prior to the arrival of Celestina, the servant describes the old madame to Calisto in the following terms: "Ella tenía seis oficios, conviene saber: labrandera, perfumera, maestra de hacer afeites y de hacer virgos, alcahueta y un poquito hechicera." The portrait Párrmeno draws of the old dame is unusually accurate with reference to the reality Rojas has given her in his work. Indeed, the image of Dame Celestina which her author brings forward throughout his composition is that of an old retired prostitute too far past her prime to participate any longer. The reader is taken a-whoring through Celestina's pleasure palace into the chambers where the 'oldest profession' is practiced. In short, Rojas has richly re-created the seamy world of illicit *erotica* at the center of which stands the compelling, if morally tarnished, figure of Celestina.

This is the ever-present background into which the love of Calisto and Melibea descends. The hero's passion degenerates into lust with the help of Celestina's skills. She is, as Pármeno indicates, first a flesh merchant and only incidentally, if at all, a witch. At least Rojas does not emphasize this dimension, although he does refer to it from time to time. Even if he did envision his immortal creation primarily as a witch, he certainly was not aware that her death at the hands of Calisto's servants was inconsistent with current ideas concerning the ability of witches to foresee the course of future events. Celestina did not count on this accident, as any legitimate witch most surely would have done.

Lope's Fabia is only a reminiscence of Celestina. The lusty background of fleshy revels, the bawdy house, the girls in the employ of Celestina, the long history of successful 'business,' the entire cellar of society's subterranean sector is notoriously absent from the *Caballero*. That Fabia is an *alcahueta* Lope leaves to his spectator's recall of Celestina. The emphasis which Pármeno placed on the professional credentials of Calisto's go-between is diminished, in Lope's play, in favor of the last office that the servant mentioned. The dramatic image that Fabia projects is more akin to Gerarda's of *La Dorotea* in that on the surface she gives the impression of an old busybody clandestinely and quite officiously arranging young love matches. But the *Caballero* is a play, not a novel, and the presence on stage of Fabia is correlated throughout with the dark atmosphere which progressively descends upon the action, rendering her figure immeasurably more affective than a character in a novel. The temptation to see in her only the reflection of Celestina is a danger inherent in all *terceras* subsequent to Rojas's unforgettable creation, especially if the pander under consideration is obliged to remain imprisoned in the printed page. But Fabia on stage, conditioning the histrionic reality of the *Caballero*, cuts quite a different figure on the slate of contemporary sensitivities and superstitions. In the weave of uncommon occurrences distributed throughout the action, the theater-goer of the day would have recognized in Fabia what Marcela knows of Teodora:

> Cerca de San Sebastián
> vive esa dueña de honor,

3. ALCAHUETERÍA AND BRUJERÍA

> con su poco de color
> y sus tocas de azafrán.
>
> Es mujer de escapulario
> con más botes de virtudes,
> aguas, yerbas y saludes
> que hay en cas del boticario.
>
> *Es, diferenciando el centro*
> *de aquella exterior esfera,*
> *ermitaña por de fuera*
> *y demonio por de dentro.*
> (*El acero de Madrid*, BAE, XXIV, 375-c.
> Italics mine.)

Whether or not Lope himself believed in witches and their arts cannot be answered. From the discussion to follow it should become clear that Medieval and Renaissance Europe certainly did take the witch most seriously. And Lope wrote the *Caballero* for the audiences of his day. Aside from this, however, it should be pointed out that the Fabia of this tragedy is not the only Fabia we find in the sundry works of the *Fénix*. The "Egloga a Amarilis" assumes an unusual importance at this point. The affair with Amarilis (Marta de Nevares), perhaps the most inflamed of all Lope's amorous pursuits, ended in bizarre tragedy. First the beautiful green eyes were suddenly afflicted with blindness, and subsequently Marta lost her mind. Shortly thereafter she passed forever from the arms of the grief-stricken poet. In the "Egloga," Lope accounts for what might have been a cerebral hemorrhage, as the "hechizos y conjuros" of one of his former lovers, herself insane with jealousy, who called forth the "espíritus fieros" to deal with her rival and thus avenge herself on Elisio (Lope). Toward the end of the poem the shepherd compares the former lover with Circe and Medea, commonly regarded in the Renaissance as the most notorious witches of Antiquity. Interestingly, Tello compares Fabia to the same two classical figures in Act III. (815-b.) The most arresting feature of the "Egloga," however, is the name which Lope assigns to his malefactress, none other than Fabia. Elisio tells his listeners that the death of his Amarilis occurred ten years before the time of his narration. (199-b.) Now, Lope composed the "Egloga" in 1633, one year after the real death of Marta. If the shepherd's remark has any meaning at all, the date 1622 or 23 (ten years from the death or the time of composition) becomes significant. Morley and Bruerton believe the *Caballero* was written between 1620 and 1625. Is it possible that in 1633, when Lope recreated the love affair with Amarilis, he recalled a similar Fabia of approximately ten years earlier? To be sure, both Fabias do indeed bring about, through their sinister science, the death of a lover.

If one is ever to understand the art of the old masters he must first submerge himself in the traditions which were the leaven of their bread. In the scholar's tireless quest to reconstruct the moral, theological, and aesthetic ideals of yesteryear, on the assumption that man defines his history in terms of positive construction, too little ink has been dedicated to man's failures. Beneath the record of brilliant achievement lies a bedrock of human inertia and shortcomings. However creative the Renaissance might have been, the fact remains that one of Europe's saddest chapters was written during the age of Cervantes, Martin Luther, Santa Teresa, Suárez, Descartes and all the illustrious spirits through which the Age of Genius is described. Rome persecuted its Christians and the Renaissance its witches. If the universe was illuminated by the flame of intelligence that was unlike any that history had known before, its heavens were also blackened by the soot of witch burnings. *Convicta et combusta* was the short legal phrase that recorded the death of countless individuals who had the misfortune to have been born with a supernumerary nipple or a prominent skin blemish. The belief in witchcraft was as much a part of the social tissue from the fifteenth through the eighteenth centuries as the bewildering array of political 'isms' is characteristic of the nineteenth and twentieth. That witchcraft was the *bête noire* of the Renaissance is at best a courteous understatement.

What, then, was witchcraft, and what was the popular image of the witch? The diabolical science was the cult or religion of those who renounced the Christian God and swore allegiance to Satan, who became their deity. In return for this apostasy Lucifer's followers were granted special powers and privileges denied to ordinary human beings. Knowledge of, and participation in, the black arts betrays a desire to acquire power and control over the normal processes of nature by which the universe is regulated. Witchcraft is magic oriented toward a destructive rather than a constructive principle. Implicit in its philosophy is a fundamental dualism that divides the cosmos into a sphere of light and a sphere of darkness, and between these two metaphysical components there can exist only eternal antagonism. If Christianity was the theological center of the light, witchcraft was its counterpart in the demon's kingdom. Christ and Lucifer, the Prince of Virtue and the monarch of evil, assume within this conception the roles of warlord and deliverer to the faithful of each. Metaphysically considered, witchcraft was Christianity turned inside out. Or so it would seem from the accounts we have of it during the Renaissance.[1]

Witchcraft, understood within a social and psychological perspective, can be defined in another manner. Every society needs an explanation for evil that is more concrete than the abstract and abstruse principles offered by its dominant philosophies or theologies. Perhaps more than explanation, what is called for is a material focal point toward which man can project all that he holds to be perverse, repugnant, destructive and opposed to righteousness. It is one thing to define evil as the absence of light, but somehow Augustine's reasoning did not satisfy the latent hostility of a medieval farmer toward a neighbor whose flourishing crops only aggravated his attitude, especially when his own cabbages and barley were withering. Either God was punishing the serf — and this alternative, of course, meant recognizing the plaintiff's own shortcomings — or the neighbor was enjoying prosperity because of a secret entente with the devil, or perhaps a third party had blighted the crops. The last two alternatives were more comfortable because they explained the phenomenon and justified the farmer's expressing his envy as Christian indignation. If the neighbor could be accused of witchcraft all that was unchristian in the laborer's spirit could be conveniently imputed to this servant of Satan, and thus made public and objective in the name of service to Christ. Philosophers and theologians can be content with a principle and theory of evil; the less intellectually gifted, however, demand an enemy to complement the abstraction. Unlike Augustine, most men do not have the courage to confess the presence of a dark sector in their souls.

---

[1] The reader is referred to the bibliography for a listing of various outstanding studies of the witchcraft phenomenon.

During the span of the great witch hysteria, there was little if any grasp of the unconscious mind as we understand it. In a social and spiritual order which recognized only consciousness and reason, and had declared the Bacchanalia and Saturnalia to be pagan and sordid celebrations irreconcilable with the Christian way, the onus of individual moral responsibility became crushing. Extreme moral transgression was either an unutterable wantonness, a depravity which for modesty's sake could only be alluded to, or else a clear case of diabolical possession. In either dimension the violation had to be understood with reference to a framework of conscious objectivity, and the responsibility for it was directed either to the transgressor or the witch. Since there was no theory of the unconscious, in the modern sense, to provide an acceptable release, both amoral and 'aresponsible,' for the destructive coefficient in man's nature, the axiological system was precariously balanced between reward or punishment, orthodoxy or heresy, virtue or sin, in short, Christ or Lucifer, as Aldous Huxley demonstrated in his admirable study of the demoniacal possession at Loudun.[2] In the discovery of witchcraft the means of coping with the devil and casting out his demons had indeed been found! In one of those peculiar inversions of the mind to which *homo sapiens* is often subject, the malefactors became not the effect of man's limitations, but rather the cause of all that was mysterious, unexplainable, shameless, and evil. The witch during the fifteenth, sixteenth, and seventeenth centuries was the instrument through which the responsibility for the destructive forces present in all creation was transferred from the individual to another source in order to fix blame somewhere. Thus she functioned much the same as the Jews did in the Third Reich, the capitalists in Russia, or the communists in America today. She was the center of subversion, the enemy of the people, a menace to the faith, an omnipresent danger to 'our way of life,' the hideous specter of what 'they would do if they took over,' etc., etc.; in brief, the aggregate perversion and cussedness which any scapegoat represents.

---

[2] Aldous Huxley, *The Devils of Loudun* (New York, 1952). See especially Chapter VII of this engrossing study.

3. ALCAHUETERÍA AND BRUJERÍA

The sinister world in which these horrendous old hags operated, a remarkable creation of the popular phantasy, was indeed a dismal portrait of awesome characteristics. The witches were usually women, although male witches were not entirely unknown. In return for voluntary worship of the demon, the archfiend had bestowed upon them certain transcendental powers. They could blight crops and livestock, control the weather and thus create storms, floods, fires, cause disturbances in the order of nature and create unreal illusions reminiscent of those created by don Juan Manuel's Deán of Santiago. They were believed to possess faculties of prevision which enabled them to foretell the exact course of future events. (One wonders how it was, therefore, that so many were apprehended by the civil authorities, apparently in total ignorance that they were even suspected of *maleficium,* let alone in danger of arrest.) Particularly terrifying was their ability to induce inordinate lust, cause bodily sickness, produce sterility in both sexes, paralyze the will, and generally do grievous harm to the person of their victims. Since witches were armed with such an arsenal of wicked capabilities, is it any wonder that the mere mention of them cast the more credulous into mild hysteria and sent the less gullible at least in search of their rosaries?

If the unnatural powers that the witches were supposed to possess were repugnant to contemplate, their personal habits and religious practices were even more loathsome. It was widely believed that they belonged to a local organization known as a coven, the number in each varying from area to area. To celebrate Satan's lordship and render homage to him, they would gather from time to time in isolated places throughout Europe: Spanish and French witches were especially fond of the Pyreness. Such an event — the witches' sabbat — was an occasion which demanded no small preparation on their part. To arrive at the appointed place they had to anoint their bodies with a concoction compounded of the most repulsive ingredients. The purpose of this ritual was to enable them to take flight through the air on a staff which would transport them to their rendezvous. The witches themselves believed that Lucifer was present at the sabbat (or *aquelarre,* as the Basque and Navarrese malefactors knew it) in the form of a goat. As good Christians kissed the hand of the bishop, the witches expressed their devotion to the devil by kissing his fundament. Satan's anatomy, even in his goat-like form, was peculiar in that beneath his tail was another face complete with eyes, lips, etc. The celebration of the black mass was the real purpose of these nocturnal meetings. It appears to have been a parody of the Christian mass. The sign of the cross, for example, was described upside down, from the bottom up, and with the left hand. The devout were sprinkled liberally with urine *in nomine diaboli* as the counterpart of holy water. After the mass, each of the witches communed with the demon, not spiritually but in the flesh. Renaissance witch trials are filled with accounts of copulation of the prince of darkness with all his faithful, the immense size and unusual coldness of his privates, and the excruciating pain which this experience occasioned. I shall spare my reader any further elaboration of the wretched ceremonies connected with the *aquelarres*. Cervantes has left a vivid portrait of the witch in his *Coloquio de los perros* to which the more curious reader is referred. Enough has been said to provide an insight into the revolting and terrifying figure that the hag evoked in the popular mind. William West, writing shortly before 1594, defines and describes her in a tone half-indignant, half-frightened:

> A witch or hag is she which being eluded by a league made with the devil through his persuasion, inspiration and juggling, thinketh she can design what manner of evil things soever, either by thought or imprecation, as to shake the air with lightinings and thunder, to cause hail and tempests, to remove green corn or trees to another place, to be carried of her familiar which hath taken upon him the deceitful shape of a goat, swine or calf, etc., in some mountain far distant, in a wonderful short space of time, and sometimes fly upon a staff or fork, or some other instrument. And to spend all the night after with her sweetheart, in playing, sporting, banqueting, dancing, dalliance, and diverse other devlish lusts and lewd disports, and to show a thousand such mockeries. [3]

There is perhaps no more convenient and convincing method of demonstrating the reality of the witch belief than to examine

---

[3] William West, *Symbolaegraephie* (London, 1594), in Christine Hole, *A Mirror of Witchcraft* (London, 1957), 25.

3. ALCAHUETERÍA AND BRUJERÍA

briefly its history from the Middle Ages through the seventeenth century. Since the purpose of this survey is to re-create for the contemporary student of Lope's theater the essentials of an outlook, the architecture of a tradition, so to speak, which the dramatist inherited, the following portion will limit itself primarily to the Iberian scene. Witchcraft in Spain, especially during the period of the panic, presents a somewhat different picture —at least on the surface— from its development in other areas of the Continent. In France, Scotland, England, Germany, Sweden, the Low Countries, and Italy, the witch preoccupation burst forth into a virtual epidemic bordering on what can best be described as a national psychosis. [4] Witch hunts, the trials, the burnings, the professional 'discoverers,' all conspired in these nations to fan the heat of hysteria, thus touching off a new round of activity. The mere suspicion of a pact with the devil was enough to occasion an accusation, indictment, arrest, trial, and frequently certain death by mob violence on the spot, so intense and widespread was the popular craze. In the brief chronicle of the goetic science which follows it will be demonstrated that although Spain did not suffer the witch plagues that spread through the rest of Europe, the belief in the presence of the devil's legions was no less rooted in the soil south of the Pyrenees than elsewhere.

The early Church, according to a somewhat mysterious utterance known as the *Canon episcopi* pronounced any and all belief in Diana's diabolical cult to be relics of paganism, illusion and false doctrine encouraged by the devil amongst the gullible. [5] Those who placed credence in witch flights and gatherings were directed to undertake penance for their heretical inclinations. This document, supposed to have been the work of an unauthenticated Council of Anquira in the fourth century, today is held to date from no earlier than the ninth. Whatever the *ab quo* and *ad quem* dates of the *Canon* may be, it does reflect the presence during the early Middle Ages of individuals who accepted the witch reality. The compilers of the *Fuero juzgo*, to judge by the harsh punishments they prescribed for sorcerers, necromancers, divines, etc., did

---

[4] For accounts of witchcraft in these countries see H. C. Lea, *Materials Towards a History of Witchcraft* (Philadelphia, 1939).

[5] See J. Caro Baroja, *Las brujas y su mundo* (Madrid, 1961), 98.

not subscribe to the theory of illusion which the *Canon episcopi* advocated, but, of course, the *Fuero* may well be the earlier compilation. From these texts alone it becomes clear that a legal and ecclesiastical preocupation with malefactors manifested itself in Europe and Spain when the modern world was still virtually in its infancy.

Alfonso el Sabio did not regard magic and the occult sciences as arts which were necessarily heretical. In the *Partida VII, título xxiii, ley 3,* he distinguishes carefully between the activities of the black witches and evil doers, who should be put to death forthwith, and white witches "...que ficiesen encantamientos o otras cosas con buena entension," in return for which services, the law continues, "...antes decimos que deven recebir galardón por ello." For Alfonso, at least, there appears to be not the slightest hesitancy concerning whether or not sorcerers and their kind represented a temptation of the demon set before the minds of men. Nor do the implications of the *Canon* deter Jacobo de las Leyes from affirming that those individuals who cause death through the operation of some secret enchantment must be classified with the most notorious malefactors.[6] Despite the awareness, however, on the part of medieval jurists that persons skilled in the black arts were a fact of life, there appears to be no indication of any widespread hysteria occasioned by their presence. Until about the middle of the fourteenth century, the *saludadoras, ensalmadoras, entendederas,* and *alcahuetas,* primarily of Jewish and Moorish origin, went about their business relatively unencumbered by the horrid reputation they were to acquire within fifty years.

The first indication of a change in the climate of opinion occurs in Southern France. The earliest known reference to the witch sabbat is found in the records of the Carcassone trials that took place between 1330 and 1340.[7] This event is of cardinal importance to the future development of the ideas surrounding witchcraft. The witches have now become organized into a kind of international Mafia under the leadership of Beelzebub, consciously and

---

[6] See *Flores de las leyes* in *Memorial histórico español* (Madrid, 1851), II, 243.

[7] See Joseph Hansen, *Zauberwahn, Inquisition und Hexenprozes im Mittelalter und die Entstehung der grossen Hexenverfolgung* (München-Leipzig, 1900), 315.

directly opposed to the Church and the well-being of Christian society. The sabbat had no other purpose than to bring these perverted souls together in one place and at one time to be instructed in the goetic arts. The legal proceedings against witches during this decade are inextricably implicated in the Church's struggle against the Cathar heresy then rampant in all of the Midi, and the trials of these witches are curiously related to the world of Cathar dualism.[8] As the Cathari had been accused of kissing Satan in the form of a cat or frog, so the witches now, in the sabbat, were said to kiss the fundament of the lord of the underworld.[9] Catharism had been declared a heresy of the vilest sort, and since 1230, the Church had been locked in deadly battle with the cult of the Pure. Guilt by association, if nothing more, was sufficient to place those accused of the dark science in an untenable and dangerous position for which, given the temper of the times, there was little likelihood of adequate defense. By the middle of the fifteenth century, the victory over Catharism was all but complete, but the passions the struggle had aroused were still glowing white hot. It is no accident, therefore, that the appearance of the witch epidemic coincides with the destruction of the hated Provençal heresy, especially since sorcery and Catharism itself had been linked together. In a sense, the momentum which the Cathar conflagration had generated was simply transferred to a new enemy, a more deadly and treacherous foe who operated 'underground,' and thus a new crusade was launched against the devil's saboteurs.

During the latter third of the fourteenth century the signs of a growing anxiety become clearer. By 1370 a law enacted by Enrique III accuses all persons who are discovered consulting diviners guilty of heresy and punishable accordingly. In 1387, Juan I reiterates the charge of heresy promulgated by his royal predecessor. From this date through the early years of the fifteenth century the activity associated with the black science appears to increase considerably, for on April 9, 1414, a *pragmática* was handed down which set severe penalties on transgressors and prescribed judicial responsibilities in unequivocal language.

---

[8] Hansen, *Zauberwahn*, 315.
[9] Hansen, *Zauberwahn*, 214-234.

As the climate of apprehension became more pronounced, so also did the witchcraft question reflect itself anew in various forms throughout the fifteenth century. Whereas prior to this period in Spain, the occult arts and their practitioners from time to time came to the attention of the lawmakers, a renewed interest in this area by the more theologically and philosophically oriented brains of the day can be noted. Alonso de Madrigal and Lope de Barrientos return to the *Canon episcopi* as the document from which all discussion must depart. For the latter, in his *Tratado de la adevinanza*, the notion that witches can fly through the air and can cause damage is, "fablando teologalmente," the work of evil spirits that conjure up "diversas especies e figuras" in the minds of their victims. The reality of a battalion of old hags wickedly attending an *aquelarre* is pure phantasy, "e cualquiera que lo creyere," he affirms, "es infiel e peor que pagano." [10] Despite these learned disputations, or perhaps because of them, witchcraft in the fifteenth century had achieved a condition of firm belief in the popular mind, the *Canon* notwithstanding. The very fact that Barrientos gallantly discourses against what to him appears a ridiculous absurdity for logical and authoritative reasons is an indication that witches had become an issue.

Social conditions elsewhere on the Continent during the early part of the fifteenth century were to cast a sinister shadow over Spain. In order to reconstruct the full force of the witch sensitivity in the sixteenth and seventeenth centuries in the Peninsula, it is essential to digress for a moment to examine events taking place in Northern Germany. There the clergy and the civil arm had been for some time in the midst of an outbreak of popular hysteria that had reached epidemic proportions. There had been two notorious witch burnings in Heidelberg (1446) and Cologne (1456). So extensive was the panic that it came to the attention of the Pope, Innocent VIII, who, in 1484, issued what was to be perhaps the most important of all documents affecting the development of European consciousness with regard to witchcraft. The Papal Bull "Summis desiderantes affectibus" was directed to the German clergy as a kind of letter of introduction for two Domi-

---

[10] J. Caro Baroja, *Las brujas*, 165.

3. ALCAHUETERÍA AND BRUJERÍA

nican Inquisitors, Henry Krämer and Joseph Sprenger who, in their investigations and travels, apparently had met with considerable hostility on the part of some prelates and civil officials. The Bull expressly authorizes and gives papal sanction to these two representatives to ferret out and prosecute all of Satan's minions, male and female, a duty they discharged, as will be shown, with remarkable zeal. Innocent's directive to the North German brethren is particularly noteworthy because it appears to recognize fully and with no reservations the reality of witchcraft, *thus seemingly affirming the whole complex of popular superstition as enjoying papal support*. This paragraph is of such importance to the development of the witch frenzy that it deserves quotation:

> It has indeed lately come to Our ears, not without afflicting Us with bitter sorrow, that in some parts of Northern Germany, as well as in the provinces, townships, territories, districts, and diocesis of Mainz, Cologne, Treves, Salzburg, and Bremen, many persons of both sexes, unmindful of their own salvation and straying from the Catholic Faith, have abandoned themselves to devils, incubi and succubi, and by their incantations, spells, conjurations, and other accursed charms and crafts, enormities and horrid offences, have slain infants yet in the mother's womb, as also the offspring of cattle, have blasted the produce of the earth, the grapes of the vines, the fruits of the trees, nay, men and women, beasts of burthen, herd-beasts, as well as animals of other kinds, vineyards, orchards, meadows, pastureland, corn, wheat, and all other cereals; these wretches furthermore afflict and torment men and women, beasts of burthen, herd-beasts, as well as animals of other kinds with terrible and piteous pain and sore diseases, both internal and external; they hinder men from performing the sexual act and women from conceiving, whence husbands cannot know their wives nor wives receive their husbands; over and above this, they blasphemously renounce that Faith which is theirs by the Sacrament of Baptism, and at the instigation of the Enemy of mankind they do not shrink from committing and perpetrating the foulest abominations and filthiest excesses to the deadly peril of their own souls, whereby they outrage the Divine Majesty and are a cause of scandal and danger to very many.[11]

---

[11] In H. Krämer and J. Sprenger, *Malleus maleficarum*, trans. Montague Summers (London, 1951), xix-xx.

No better definition and portrait of the witch was to emerge from the Renaissance, not even that of Cervantes in *El coloquio de los perros*, than this by none other than a Roman Catholic Pope. Whether or not Innocent intended his remarks as a flat contradiction of the *Canon* may never be resolved. What is certain, however, is that after two years, when Krämer and Sprenger completed their mission, they published the notorious *Malleus maleficarum* to which they appended the Bull. The effect of this inclusion was to give a singularly strong impression to the uncritical reader that their study not only enjoyed papal approval, but also authorization for the procedures it describes.

The *Malleus* itself is a vast compendium of every folk belief conceivable surrounding the witch phenomenon. It is divided into three parts as follows: Part I, "Treating of the Three Necessary Concomitants of Witchcraft which are the Devil, a Witch, and the Permission of Almighty God." Here the good brothers affirm with not the slightest hesitation the existence of witches, their practices, their commerce with Satan, and their guilt, all "scientifically demonstrated" with abundant cases drawn from experience and eye witness accounts. Part II bears the title, "Treating of the Methods by which the Works of Witchcraft are Wrought and Directed, and how they may be Successfully Annulled and Dissolved," in which the indisputable truth of Part I is further reinforced. It is the Third Part that, as far as the history of witchcraft is concerned, was to have the saddest repercussions throughout Europe. It is entitled, "Relating to the Judicial Proceedings in Both the Ecclesiastical and Civil Courts against Witches and Indeed all Heretics." All of the machinery of trial, indictment, and judgement are detailed in cold and impersonal language. Hearsay evidence, testimony of children and the enemies of the accused are sanctioned, together with torture. It is here that the beginnings of the dread legal *petitio principii* are set forth. The accused had no defense because of the nature of the accusation. To speak up in favor of the defendant automatically branded the witness as sympathetic to the demon's designs. Thus accusation meant, for all practical purposes, judgement. With the appearance of the *Malleus* that which had only smouldered previously now broke forth into a raging holocaust.

3. ALCAHUETERÍA AND BRUJERÍA

Almost overnight the *Malleus* became the standard authority for prosecution, especially in the civil courts. There is perhaps no more classic case of the remedy which begets more sickness which calls for more liberal dosage of the medications, etc., *ad infinitum*, than that which this treatise exemplifies. From 1486, the date of its first publication, until 1520, it went through fourteen editions. Nor did its popularity wane at this time. Four printings appeared in the seventeenth century through 1666. (*Malleus*, xviii.) The Frankfurt edition of 1588 carries with it nine separate treatises by learned authorities on witches. And, of course, throughout the sixteenth and seventeenth centuries the witch hunts erupted all over Europe from large city to small hamlet. With the *Malleus*, then, the popular image of the witch was crystallized once and for all and dignified by the prestige of two such experienced inquisitors, not to mention the 'approval' of the Pope.

From 1500 onward the face of Spanish history becomes increasingly pockmarked by the witch preoccupation. The following chronology is offered at this point by way of demonstrating the extent and frequency of the hysteria. For thorough discussions of each incidence the reader is referred to H. C. Lea,[12] M. Menéndez y Pelayo,[13] J. Caro Baroja,[14] and S. Cirac Estopañán[15] from whose researches the dates and data are principally drawn.

1500: Trial of the Sierra de Amboto region in Vizcaya. (Menéndez y Pelayo, *Heterodoxos*, II, 453. See also Caro Baroja, *Las brujas*, 212.)

1507: Twenty nine witches punished by the Inquisition of Calahorra. (Menéndez y Pelayo, *Heterodoxos*, IV, 374.)

1522: An Edict of Grace was issued to all witches of Jaca and Ribagorza to identify themselves and confess their heresy. (Lea, *A History*, IV, 211.)

---

[12] Henry Charles Lea, *A History of the Inquisition of Spain* (New York, 1907), Vol. IV.

[13] M. Menéndez y Pelayo, *Historia de los heterodoxos españoles* (Santander, 1947).

[14] J. Caro Baroja, *Las brujas*.

[15] Sebastián Cirac Estopañán, *Procesos de hechicerías en la inquisición de Castilla la nueva* (Madrid, 1942).

1526: The Assembly of Granada was convened to discuss the outbreak of extensive witch activities in Navarra. (Lea, *A History*, IV, 212.)

1527: Two girls in Pamplona confessed to being witches and were permitted to reveal to the authorities the whereabouts of all the malefactors of the region. According to Prudencio de Sandoval 150 *brujas* and *brujos* were apprehended. (Caro Baroja, *Las brujas*, 213.)

1528: Sancho de Carranza de Miranda, the Inquisitor of Calahorra, was ordered by the Inquisitor General to conduct a minute investigation of the panic in Vizcaya because the residents of that area had been reporting for some time numerous cases of damages caused by witches. (Caro Baroja, *Las brujas*, 222.)

1530: The Assembly of Fuenterrabía was convened to study ways of discovering and punishing witches. (Caro Baroja, *Las brujas*, 220.)

1535: Arnaldo Albertino and Alfonso de Castro explicitly contradict the *Canon episcopi* and affirm the reality of witchcraft. (Lea, *A History*, IV, 217.)

1538: The Inquisitor Valdeolitas was sent to Navarra with instructions to combat the popular demand that all accused witches be burnt at the stake, and further to convince the more educated that natural catastrophes were not always due to the spells of witches and to inform the civil authorities that the *Malleus* was not to be believed in every particular. (Lea, *A History*, IV, 219.)

1555: Several cities of Guipúzcoa demanded that the Inquisition mete out punishment to their witches. (Caro Baroja, *Las brujas*, 221.)

1555-58: Notorious case of the trials of Celeberio during which one family accused another of being a coven. Like the 1527 affair, the civil authorities admitted the evidence of small children. Twenty one persons were arrested. (Caro Baroja, *Las Brujas*, 221.)

1575: A new epidemic swept Navarra. The civil magistrates demanded "exemplary punishment" for the many individuals in their prisons. (Caro Baroja, *Las brujas*, 223.)

1595: Tolosa declared a discovery of witches. (Caro Baroja, *Las brujas*, 223.)

1598: At the convocation of the Cortes in Madrid the terror had grown to such proportions that the *procuradores* from cities

3. ALCAHUETERÍA AND BRUJERÍA

and towns throughout the Kingdom petitioned Phillip II to issue a decree categorically prohibiting occult practices, white or black. The King, in turn, declared an immediate invigoration of all precedent statutes and laws associated with witchcraft. [16]

1600: Román Ramírez, the famous necromancer from Deza, was tried and convicted. [17]

1610: The trial of Logroño. Of all the witch incidents this one is perhaps the most memorable. An entire sect of warlocks and witches had been exposed in Zugarramurdi. The proceedings were opened to the public. The Auto de Logroño is the classical example of hysterical stimulation brought on by the legal machinery intended to eradicate the evil. [18] After the spectacle was concluded, one of the Inquisitors, Adolfo de Salazar y Frías, who had been very dubious about the confessions and the nature of the legal procedures, was commissioned by the Suprema to carry out further inquiries in the Logroño region. His report is a masterpiece of the anatomy of group hysteria and human credulousness. [19]

1611: A trial was held in Fuenterrabía to prosecute a known practitioner of the black arts. (Caro Baroja, *Las brujas*, 272.)

1621: Diego de Irarraga, Señor de Iraeta, called upon the Inquisition to bring action against the witches of Guipúzcoa. (Caro Baroja, *Las brujas*, 271.)

1622: The first witch's laboratory was discovered in Madrid in the quarters of one Josefa Carranza. Among the effects was a human skull. (Cirac Estopañán, *Procesos*, 40.) As has been noted before, the *Caballero de Olmedo*, according to Morley and Bruerton, was probably written between 1620 and 1625.

---

[16] José Amador de los Ríos, "De las artes mágicas y de adivinación en el suelo ibérico," *Revista de España*, XVIII, 332-333.

[17] See Martín del Río's account of the trial in his *Disquisitionum magicarum libri sex* (Venice, 1616), lib. II, quaest. 24. Ramírez is the protagonist of Alarcón's *Quien mal anda mal acaba*.

[18] See also Caro Baroja, *Las brujas*, Chapters XIII and XIV.

[19] See *Relacion y epilogo de lo que a resultado de la visita q hizo el sancto offi° en las montañas del Rey° de Navarra y otras partes con el hedito de gracia concedido a los que ouiesen ycurrido en la secta de Brujos conforme a las relaciones que de todo ello se an Remitido al Consejo*, in *Anuario de Ausko Folklore*, XII, 115-130.

1627: Ana de Jodar, María de San León, and Francisca Méndez declared to be sorceresses in the Auto de Córdoba. (Lea, *A History*, IV, 197.)

1630: A circle of devil worshippers was discovered in Cuenca headed by Cristóbal Chirinos, among whose members was an unfrocked Dominican. (Cirac Estopañán, *Procesos*, 277-278.)

1631: Fr. Juan Ponce de León denounced the contraband traffic of forbidden books dealing with magic, sorcery, necromancy, etc., usually printed in Toulouse, Antwerp, Venice, and other European cities. Designated as an arch offender was one Pedro Mallar, a French national, "inclinado a judiciario y al arte de alzar figura. No se vacía su casa todo el día de judiciarios ni de hombre de este humor." (Cirac Estopañán, *Procesos*, 36.) [20]

1633: Antonia Mejía de Acosta, a notorious witch and *alcahueta*, was tried before the Tribunal de Toledo. Doña Antonia was held to be an *hechicera de hechiceras*, who was widely reputed to have had no equal in all of New Castile "por su saber amatorio." She was a "natural de Madrid." (Cirac Estopañán, *Procesos*, 136.)

1639: Bárbara de Olmedo and her daughter, María, were accused of practicing the black arts in El Toboso. (Cirac Estopañán, *Procesos*, 46.)

1656: The famous "bruja y alcahueta madrileña," la Margaritona, was arrested in the Casa de las Siete Chimeneas. She was publicly exhibited throughout the city and sentenced to death. La Margaritona, like Antonia Mejía de Acosta, her predecessor, seems to have enjoyed unusual renown as a love merchant and procuress. She was 88 years of age; thus, at the time of the probable composition of Lope's play she was in her fifties. [21]

The objective of this modest chronology, which is by no means complete, is to establish several perspectives: 1) the extent of the witch preoccupation both temporally and geographically in Spain of the sixteenth and seventeenth centuries; and 2) the presence, in the capital, of witch incidents not only during the period in

---

[20] According to Cirac Estopañán, the *Malleus* was known in Spain from the end of the fifteenth century; see *Procesos*, 250.

[21] José Deleitó y Piñuela, *La mala vida en la España de Felipe II* (Madrid, 1948), 71-74.

which Lope's play was written, but in that following its composition as well. It was against the background of this social reality that the audiences of the day witnessed the tragedy of the Knight from Olmedo. The following examination of Lope's fascinating match-maker sets out from an angle of vision that reflects the social ambient outlined above. Her portrait, as the dramatist has painted it, is a study in light and shadow.

Like tragedy itself, Fabia has two faces. To the hero and heroine she is a kindly old *medianera* who earns her keep by arranging secret meetings for love-sick youths and maidens. They can see in her only the mask of love's adjutant, since this is the facet of her character that she turns toward them. But Lope, it must be remembered, created his *alcahueta* during the years when la Margaritona was active in Madrid, and the law was busy ferreting out accused witches and discovering their laboratories. Throughout the tragedy, the *Fénix* repeatedly directs the spectator's eye to the face beneath the mask, to the devil's mark buried within the wrinkled countenance and concealed by the cosmetics that she peddles. The signs that delineate the shape of a witch are distributed at regular intervals in the play, and communicate another surface of the stage reality. To an audience sensitive to this social tradition, Fabia's figure was unmistakable. Lope reveals her true office in several ways: by what she says, by what is said about her, by what she does; thus we are invited to believe that what happens in the play, especially in the third Act, is in some mysterious way related to her franchise with Lucifer.

The clues Lope sets forth concerning the identification of Fabia's other side appear with greatest frequency in Act I. It is here that the sinister image must be developed if her shadow is to fall over all that takes place in subsequent developments. The first indication that there is more to her than meets the eye occurs during her initial meeting with Alonso. She has just promised to alleviate the pain of his infirmity.

> ALONSO: ¿Con qué te podré pagar
> la vida, el alma que espero,
> Fabia, de esas santas manos?
> TELLO: ¿Santas?
> ALONSO: ¿Pues no, si han de hacer
> milagros?
> TELLO: De Lucifer. (795-b.)

Alonso, paralyzed by his infatuation, regards her as a veritable priestess *(santas manos)* of love's cult delivered to him for his salvation. Tello, representing the more 'objective' view, knows only too well that her beatitude originates from her membership in Satan's church. The discrepancy of vision between Alonso and Tello points up the ambivalence of Fabia's portrait which Lope projects toward his audience. It is thus, in this bipartite configuration of Fabia that the residing irony of Alonso's remark, "si han de hacer milagros," is felt, because miracles indeed will occur in Act III, but of quite another sort than those the hero expects. The discourse at this point is enough to arouse a suspicion of multiple perspectives with reference to Fabia's identity.

Some 47 lines later, as Fabia awaits at the door of Inés's house, she pointedly directs an *aparte* at the audience:

> Y ¡cómo si yo sabía
> que me habías de llamar! (796-a.)

And again, referring to don Pedro, Inés's father, she remarks in an aside: "Tarde vendrá." The lines are reminiscent of Celestina's first visit to Melibea's abode. But between the time that Rojas wrote and Lope's day, the great European witch hysteria had developed. The latter's public was not dissimilar from the crowds that gathered in 1610 at Logroño to witness the trials that had made that city momentarily famous, and among the accusations the populace heard was the terrifying revelation that the *xorguinas*, because of their pact with the demon, enjoyed his powers of foreknowledge. Elsewhere Lope tells us directly that the *alcahueta* clearly could predict the patterns of the future. Leonor, of *La noche de San Juan*, describes the old hag whom don Juan sent to win her affections:

> Don Juan, como pescador
> que al pez el sedal alarga
> cuando ya le rinde asido
> y va mudando la caña,
> envióme una mujer,
> de éstas que cuentan por habas
> los sucesos por venir.[22]

---

[22] In Lope de Vega, *Obras*, Nueva edición de la Real Academia Española (Madrid, 1916-1930), IX, 632-5; hereafter abbreviated NRAE.

3. ALCAHUETERÍA AND BRUJERÍA

Thus Fabia's asides at this point serve as a powerful stimulus to the popular mind to associate her with the figure of the witch. Indeed, as the play develops, Fabia's clairvoyance becomes increasingly more patent.

Once she has gained entrance to Inés's home, Lope again affixes to his dialogue a direct reference to her *maleficium*. When Inés asks her what she has brought in her basket, Fabia replies: "Papeles son / de alcanfor y solimán." (797-a.) *Solimán* is corrosive sublimate (mercuric chloride), a highly poisonous and deadly preparation that was used occasionally as a cosmetic because of its great whiteness. It is particularly toxic when applied to the skin. Concerning the chemical, Covarrubias says: "El padre Guadix dize que en arábigo vale tósigo; lo mesmo es cerca de nosotros por su mala calidad y mortífero efecto." [23] Andrés Laguna's description of *azogue* and *solimán* is unusually pertinent in understanding the symbolic properties of Fabia's *afeite*:

> Házese también del mesmo [azogue] por via de sublimation, aquel pernicioso veneno, que se dize solimán en Castilla y Argentum vinum sublimatum, en la lengua latina. El cual es no menos corrosiuo y agudo, que el mesmo fuego: por donde en algunas partes le dan fuego muerto por nombre. Del solimán se prepara una muy famosa suerte de affeyte llamada Solimán adobado. El cual tiene tanta excellentia, que las mugeres que amenudo con él se affeytan, aun que sean de pocos años, presto se tornan viejas, con vnos gestillos de monas, arrugadas y consumidas: y antes que les cargue la hedad, tiemblan las cuytadillas como azogadas, porque sin dubda lo son: visto que el Solimán solamente del azogue diffiere en esto, que es más corrosiuo y mordaz. Por donde aplicado al rostro, estirpa las senales y manchas dél. Ansí que del vso del Solimán resultan muy infames inconvenientes... Dado por la boca el Azogue es veneno mortífero, y siempre fué tenido por tal. Lo qual siendo naturalmente ansí, no se de que infernal persuasion mouidas, algunas viejas endemoniadas, le suelen dar a beuer, a las criaturas rezien nacidas, contra el alferez: o porque otra razón lo hazen, sino porque son brujas de natura y de porfession y ansí a la descubierta quieren exercitar su arte. [24]

---

[23] In *Tesoro de la lengua castellana o española* (Barcelona, 1943), 943-b.
[24] See Laguna's translation and commentary of Pedacio Dioscórides, *Acerca de la materia medicinal, y de los venenos mortíferos* (Amberes, 1555), 540-

Mercury and mercurial compounds, as Laguna indicates, were notoriously employed by Satan's minions for their diabolical preparations. The symbol of the *papeles de solimán* poetically expresses Fabia's dual role in the tragedy: it is at once a cosmetic from the House of Venus, and when applied to the skin or taken internally, a deadly corrosive poison "de mortífero efeto".

It should be noted that the texture of clues Lope has woven into his dialogue occurs with an amazing regularity throughout the first Act: approximately every fifty to eighty lines the dramatist boldly draws aside the veil of deception which separates the participants from the shadowy contours of tragedy's design. Once Inés has promised to answer the note a certain *galán* has penned to his lady, a favor to Fabia, Alonso's physician turns directly to the audience and affirms:

> Apresta
> fiero habitador del centro,
> fuego accidental que abrase
> el pecho de esta doncella. (797-b.)

This utterance is the most direct communication that Lope has addressed to his spectator up to this point. We are reminded of the effect of the *solimán* on delicate tissues, which, were Inés to apply it, would produce essentially the same result as that of the *fuego accidental* of Fabia's exhortation. The dramatist is quick to reinforce this latest revelation when Rodrigo remarks, on seeing Fabia: "Pero ¡en lugar de la mía, / aquella sombra!" (797-b.)

Perhaps the most striking demonstration of Fabia's goetic alter-image is set forth in her conversation with Tello concerning the tooth extraction. Between the exhortation and this scene Lope has briefly allowed the *gracioso* to remark to his master: "Y que Fabia fuese el ángel, / que al infierno de los palos / cayese por levantarte" (799-a.), a facetious comment that once again reminds us

---

542. Sor Juana Inés de la Cruz also comments on the deadly effect of *solimán:* "...tornasol que concita/los que del prado aplausos solicita:/ preceptor quizá vano/—si no ejemplo profano—/ de industria feminil que el más activo/veneno, hace dos veces ser nocivo/.../de la que finge tez resplandeciente." In *Obras completas,* ed. Alfonso Méndez Plancarte (Mexico, 1951), I, 354: see the editor's note, p. 600, Vol. I.

3. ALCAHUETERÍA AND BRUJERÍA

of the disparity of recognition separating Alonso from everyone else who comes in contact with the procuress. Once Alonso has left the room, all pretense of saintliness is dropped as she commands Tello to accompany her: "Una muela he menester / del salteador que ahorcaron / ayer" (800-a.), because this tooth "importa a la brevedad / deste amor." (800-a.) Horrified, Tello declines the invitation and openly accuses Fabia of possessing forbidden knowledge: "Tú, Fabia, enseñada estás / a hablar al diablo." (800-a.) To which Satan's servant replies: "Si no vas, tengo de hacer, / que él propio venga a buscarte." (800-a.) Tello quickly submits to her threat and asks: "¿Eres demonio o mujer?" (800-a.)

Fabia's need for the tooth makes a previous affirmation to Inés somewhat ironically ambiguous. In the same basket that contained the "papeles de alcanfor y solimán" there were also some "polvos de dientes." (797-a.) When we compare this article with the present scene we are forced to wonder whether the *polvos* are *para dientes* or literally made of teeth. Whereas prior to this time Lope had allowed the audience to catch only a glimpse of the face behind the mask, now he roundly confirms the hints and clues that have so regularly highlighted Fabia's delineation, with the result that the dark identity is here firmly established, and this identity, in turn, will cast its sinister coloration over the complexion of future events. Lest the modern reader be tempted to regard this interlude as "comic relief," it should be observed that in the heyday of the great witch hunts, human bones, hair, nail clippings, etc., were a common item in the necromancer's workshop, as indeed they are today where witchcraft is practiced. Lea tells us that in 1585, one Gracia Melero was publicly flogged in Zaragoza for heresy because she was discovered with the finger of a man recently hanged together with a piece of the halter. (*A History*, IV, 187.) Lope's scene is calculated to draw upon the spectator's knowledge of similar happenings and thus to shape his perception of Fabia's many skills. The invitation to ghoulish activities is not left unresolved. As Alonso waits at the *reja*, a few lines farther on, Tello informs him that he must soon depart to assist in the hellish mission. (800-b.) At the beginning of Act II, the *gracioso* relates to his *amo* what happened at the gallows (804-a.), a scene that will be discussed at a later time. And finally, there is a distant echo of the extraction later in Act II. (810-a.) Act I concludes with still another *aparte* intended for the spectators. Once Inés confesses that she is passionately enamored of Alonso, Fabia exclaims: "¡Oh, qué bravo efecto hicieron / los hechizos y conjuros! / La victoria me prometo." (802-b.) It is logically consistent with Lope's intent that the first *jornada* should not end without one more manifestation of the ambivalence integral to Fabia's character.

Other than the references to the tooth episode, Act II contains no principal direct allusions to Fabia's *maleficium*. The artistic reasons for this lack will be examined when we study the play's structure and morphology. It is enough to point out that the very absence of dramatic comment about her in Act II seems to bespeak the dramatist's confidence that the elaboration already established would carry forward. In the final Act, however, as the pattern of events begins to assume distinct tragic proportions, the *Fénix* once again returns to an occasional, but well placed, direct remark urging the public to associate the hag's presence with the traditional conception of the witch. As Alonso returns to the bullring, it occurs to Tello that Fabia is alone. In a soliloquy which resembles a similar one in the *Celestina*, Fabia is compared to the three most notorious witches of Antiquity:

> Traigo cierto pensamiento
> para coger la cadena
> a esta vieja, aunque con pena
> de su astuto entendimiento.
> No supo Circe, Medea,
> ni Hécate, lo que ella sabe;
> ....
> Pero soy un necio;
> que sabrá que el oro precio,
> y que los años desamo,
> porque se lo ha de decir
> el de las patas de gallo. (815-b.)

It is significant that Lope should return to a mention of Fabia's prescience in the third Act at precisely the prelude to Alonso's death. And following his murder, it is this same characteristic of the necromancer to which Lope again alludes not once, but twice. Inés confesses to having experienced a mood of great sadness since Alonso's departure for Olmedo, to which Fabia replies:

3. ALCAHUETERÍA AND BRUJERÍA

> Yo pienso que mayor daño
> te espera, si no me engaño,
> como suele suceder;
> que en las cosas por venir
> no puede haber cierta ciencia. (822-b.)

The effect of this observation on a baroque audience would have been to suggest that if the *medianera* did not know what had happened, she surely had strong presentiments about the hero's inevitable demise. The last segment of her dialogue seems to be urged upon her by the fact that the remark is made directly to Inés and thus conceals from the heroine any indication of occult knowledge. In the second reference to Fabia's ambivalence, which follows almost immediately, her clairvoyance is made far more explicit: "El parabién te [Inés] doy, / (Ap.) si no es pésame después." (823-a.) But here the communication is an *aparte* rather than second person discourse; thus there is no need for a final exoneration. In sum, of the four major directive comments in the final Act, three emphasize unnatural prevision.

The most complete description of Fabia in the entire tragedy is delivered to us by Rodrigo approximately half way through the last Act:

> Fabia, que puede trasponer un monte;
> Fabia, que puede detener un río,
> y en los negros ministros de Aqueronte
> tiene, como en vasallos, señorío;
> Fabia, que deste mar, deste horizonte,
> al abrasado clima, al Norte frío
> puede llevar a un hombre por el aire,
> le da liciones; ¿hay mayor donaire? (820-a.)

Rodrigo's outburst, it should be noted, is interposed between the ghost scene and the eery appearance of the *labrador*, thus indicating that Lope has deliberately interrupted the flow of action at this point. The antagonist's anguished expostulation, placed where it is in the very center of a series of mysterious occurrences, is strategically calculated to invite the spectator's attention to this point of reference as he witnesses the fantastic events of this fateful night.

In summary, therefore, Fabia's identity in the *Caballero de Olmedo* is revealed in what she says in the asides, through the remarks Tello and Rodrigo make about her, in all that she does and the many disguises she assumes, and in what happens throughout the play. When these four factors are collated with the contemporary corpus of beliefs concerning *alcahuetas* and the devil's minions, Lope's definition of her role becomes meaningful. If he has gone to unusual lengths to inform his audience that the crone, playing her part on the stage with such traditional verve, is, in reality, Beelzebub's minister, it is because his creative insight perceived in the witch the diapason of the tragic song inherent but often unrealized in the courtly code. The dark light which emanates from Fabia's configuration will bond the complexion and atmosphere of tragedy to the surface of the courtly drama.

* * *

Such, then, is the genealogy of the legend of the Knight of Olmedo and the two traditions within which Lope has chosen to interpret his treatment of it. *Cortesía* and *brujería* are the two elements which define this masterpiece of tragedy. In the compatibility of these conventions —one literary, the other social— the prevailing irony is inherent. It will be recalled that *la courtoisie* was essentially a form of social truancy. What made it appealing and exciting to the troubadours and their subsequent literary progeny was precisely that the courtly etiquette required a passing *beyond* — but only a little beyond — the code of societal acceptability. Since passion could claim no honor within the body of Christian mores, then it could only be exalted by absenting oneself temporarily from the circle of behavior which they circumscribed. The courtly songsters may have reacted against the injunctions laid on Eros by the Church, but they did not regard their camp as inimical to the conventional one. Now, like the philosophy of courtly love, witchcraft too represents a conscious attempt to move away from the center of a prevailing axiological system. However, unlike the devotees of Venus, whose delicate world depended on a symbiotic co-existence with the rest of humankind, the warlocks aspired to remove themselves *outside of*, not merely beyond, the inner circle, and in so doing to declare war on the faithful. Hostility, not relative indifference, characterized the attitude of Lucifer's host, or, at least, so it was thought. There is, then, a common factor that links the courtly inspiration to that of the witches: both groups represent highly specialized interests that were not sanctioned by either Medieval or Renaissance society. Thus the world of the witch and that of the troubadour have between them a fundamental sympathy in that the citizens of each are 'outsiders.' Witch and poet alike have different gods, but not identical ones: both must conduct their affairs in secrecy; both seek a transcendence of human limitation; and the activities of each are implicated in passion. What distinguishes witch from songster is the distance each stands from the center of social respectability, a difference between the truant and the criminal.

If genius can be defined as a faculty for synthesis of seemingly unrelated quantities and qualities, then it follows that the achievement of unity depends on an act of creative intuition which perceives likeness in disparity. The fusion of *lo cortesano* and *lo brujeril* to form an ironic action attests to the incredible vigor of Lope's insight, since two more divergent sources of inspiration would be difficult to imagine. It should be pointed out, however, that in the figure of the Spanish *alcahueta*, as both malefactress and match-maker, tradition had provided the dramatist with the magic lens through which to see the relatedness of his background elements. Thus, in Fabia, Lope inherited the poetic nexus which adjusted the courtly treatment of his re-creation to the other dimension of tragedy, the dark side expressed in this play through the old crone's role as a witch. To the extent, therefore, that she conjoins these two forbidden and illicit worlds, that is, as she functions as the common mirror in which is reflected what is alike in both, the ironic directive of tragedy gradually emerges and assumes a formal design that is best understood as the ambivalence generated from a contrapuntal fugue of love and death. If we recall for a moment the late medieval *Danza de la muerte* simultaneously with Rodrigo Cota's *Diálogo entre un viejo y el amor*, in which Love forces the old man to dance to his tune, a similarity of conception and execution can be clearly seen. Love, like Death, is no respecter of person, station, or age. Each surprises his victim when he least expects it, and both are received as unwanted visitors whose mission is to destroy peace of mind and tranquility of spirit. The individual who is ambushed by either, is seen to be utterly helpless in the presence of his powerful host. And finally, in both poems, the scene is set forth as a dance in which the poor victim sooner or later must participate, however much he resists, while the uninvited partner cruelly mocks his prey. It is interesting to observe, as Professor Edgar Wind has done, that Renaissance painters, like Lope, intuited the potential sympathy of vision in love and death, and portrayed both Cupid and the figure of Death frolicking together in the same garden.[25]

Golden Age dramatists were indeed fond of describing love as a dance and lovers as dancers. In a recent article published in *Hispanófila*,[26] I pointed out the manner in which Tirso de Molina dramatizes a love scene between a peasant girl and a young gallant in terms of a symbological dance. The procedure here is essentially one of accomodating a metaphor, a love dance, to a choreography. The transposition of poetic artifice into dramatic device is an important consideration in our understanding of Lope's treatment of the irony as it emerges from the fusion of legend and lore. In Act I, Leonor, in a gentle yet firm reprimand to her sister, comments on the nature of Alonso's intentions as she sees them: "Este galán, doña Inés, / te quiere para danzar." (799-a.) Inés's reply carries out the metaphor to its logical conclusion: "Quiere en los pies comenzar / y pedir manos después." (799-a.) As we shall see, both are correct in their appraisal of the present situation. But for the moment at least the relationship between the two lovers is a passionate one which calls for all the formal dexterity which a dance of love might demand of its participants. In order to grasp fully Leonor's innuendo, it is helpful to compare her remarks with those spoken elsewhere by other characters of Lope's creation. Ramón of *El mayor imposible* pronounces on the complexion of lovers, relating the dance metaphor to an underlying core of deceit:

---

[25] See Edgar Wind, *Pagan Mysteries in the Renaissance* (London, 1958), Chapter X, "Amor as a God of Death."

[26] "La elaboración de una escena simbológica de Tirso de Molina," *Hispanófila*, XIII, 23-32.

3. ALCAHUETERÍA AND BRUJERÍA

> Todos los amantes son
> cifra de engaños...
> Cierto poeta decía
> que eran todos los amantes
> unos vestidos danzantes
> a quien són el tiempo hacía;
> que como no es la razón
> la que ha de guiar la danza,
> no hay más duda en la mudanza
> que en hacer el tiempo el són. (BAE, XXXIV, 468-a.)

Raw passion to Trigueros of *La defensa en la verdad* is the principal motivation of lovers, and consequently their fancy pirouette bespeaks a melody of lies: "Porque abrasarse es mentir, / y el mentir toca al amante / que, con los pies de danzante, / sabe rondar y fingir." (NRAE, IV, 413-a.) It is essential to take note that love as it appears here is not related to any conjugal reference but rather to courtship and the passion which accompanies this institution. To Leonor, the hero's interest in her sister amounts to nothing more than a somewhat "dishonest" dance interlude with Inés.

If we take our cue from Lope himself, then, and envisage this love affair in its initial moments as a dance, the design of tragedy and irony begins to emerge clearly from the integration of his materials. What is initiated as a *baile de amor*, and is held to be such by the dancers and onlookers alike, is, in reality, the deceptive rhythm of quite another dance — one of death. And standing at the very center of this ambivalence is Fabia, who is at one and the same time the high priestess of Eros and Satan's nuncio on earth. In her text of the play, I. I. MacDonald reminds the reader of the various musical variations of the legend that preceded Lope's interpretation of it:

> The "Danza," as distinguished from the "Baile," where both feet and hands were used, was a dance for the feet only. From Cotarelo y Mori we learn that there was a "Danza" called "El caballero" well known in the sixteenth century, Diego Pisador mentioning it. [*Libro de música de vihuela* (1522).] Antonio de Cabezón wrote a well known set of variations on the theme of the "Caballero." The "Baile del Caballero de Olmedo" contains the refrain, together with a good number of popular tags and reminis-

> cences of early ballad catchwords. This was first published in 1617, in *Parte VII* of Lope's *comedias*, and it was assigned to him, although we have no proof that he wrote it... (MacDonald, *ed. cit.*, 111.)

Thus it is quite possible that Lope's first creative approach to the legend was expressed as a dance or inspired in one of the dance forms known in the sixteenth century.[27] In the light of this information, then, Leonor's remark to her sister is seen to be unusually helpful in appraising Lope's conception of the ironic construction of his tragedy. A dance of love which gradually evolves into one of death before our very eyes is the poetic point and counterpoint which unifies Lope's courtly treatment of the tale and his modification of Celestina from a flesh merchant to a witch.

If the tragic poem celebrates man's cognizance of a metaphysical dualism, then the solemn *anagnorisis* that finalizes this ritual attests to a universal order which is revealed as ironic, and thus tragedy depicts reality as duplex. Good and evil, illusion and substance, intention and outcome, love and death, in this view become necessarily consubstantial. Lope achieves a tragic articulation by superimposing one convention on another to create a kind of dramatic palimpsest from the integration of fundamentally conversant materials. The supreme artistic triumph of his creative intuition is that through this *montage* the paradoxical nature inherent in the logic and rhetoric of courtly love (suffering is bliss, agony is joy, living is dying, etc.) is transformed into the ambivalent vision of tragic irony. In short, in the *Caballero de Olmedo*, as elsewhere, Lope's genius distills drama from poetry. The study which follows will attempt to demonstrate, then, the *poesis* of a Spanish tragedy within the framework of reference presented in this first part.

---

[27] Emilio Cotarelo y Mori mentions several *bailes* that did indeed represent a choreography of love in one form or another. See his *Colección de entremeses, loas, bailes, jácaras y mojigangas desde fines del siglo XVI a mediados del XVIII*, in NBAE, XVII, cc-ccxxii.

PART II

PRÍNCIPE: Quien ve de lejos danzar
 al que más airoso ha sido,
 como no oye el dulce ruido
 de la música, en juzgar
    que está loco, juzga bien,
 pues sin compás las acciones
 parecen desatenciones:
 lo que no sucede a quien
    de cerca oye la armonía,
 que es alma de su primor.
 Así el que ignora de amor
 una y otra fantasía,
    a cuyo compás quien ama
 se mueve, estar loco puede
 juzgar: lo que no sucede
 a quien la dulzura inflama
    que le negó la distancia;
 pues atento al blando son,
 no oye, no mira acción
 que no le haga consonancia.
    Acércate, pues, un poco
 al ruido de amor; verás
 que está danzando a compás
 el que piensas que está loco.
          El pintor de su deshonra,
          Act I, sc. x.

ACT I

Scene one (i-ii) [1]

Alonso's opening soliloquy, like the first scene as a whole, is strikingly similar to the initial moments of the *Celestina*. Traditionally, the hero is seen on stage decrying the fact that don Amor (*ciego dios* [793-b.]), without warning, has entered his house. "De los espíritus vivos / de unos ojos procedió / este amor, que me encendió / con fuegos excesivos," he laments. (793-a.) This was in accord with another common belief in the Middle Ages and Renaissance that passionate love was a sudden infection which emanated from the eyes of the beloved, entered the body of the beholder through the same portals, and thus blighted the spirit and organism of the victim. Capellanus says:

> Love is a certain inborn suffering derived from the sight of and excessive meditation upon the beauty of the opposite sex, which causes each one to wish above all things the embraces of the other and by common desire to carry out all of love's precepts in the other's embrace. This inborn suffering comes, therefore, from seeing and meditating. Not every kind of meditation can be the cause of love, an excessive one is required; for a restrained thought does not, as a rule, return to the mind, and so love cannot arise from it. (*ACL*, 28.)

The "fuegos excesivos" of which Alonso speaks, together with the fact that the entire soliloquy informs us of unrestrained thought, indicates the presence of the amorous passion which could radically alter reason and judgement. Fabia's arrival is the first sign that the hero's behavior corresponds to the courtly canons. According to the Chaplain, once the lover has recognized the existence of passion's flame, his first thought is to engage the services of one skilled in the affairs of the heart: "...straightway he strives to get a helper, to find an intermediary." (*ACL*, 28.) Tello's brief conversation with Fabia identifies the poetic reason for her summons: Alonso is suffering from love sickness and only Doctor Fabia, as Alonso calls her ("¡Oh peregrino dotor, / y para enfermos

---

[1] Roman numerals refer to the scene divisions in the Sainz de Robles text.

de amor / Hipócrates celestial!" [794-a.]), is capable of effecting the cure. The ironic texture is felt immediately in the jubilant reception that the hero gives to the old dame. Fabia, the physician of Eros, has been invited to heal the infirmity by aggravating the infection! To the extent that Lope's bawd evokes the memory of Celestina, not to mention all of her literary progeny, she is immediately identifiable as a flesh merchant, and hence the audience recognizes the beginnings of an *amor deshonesto*.

The symptomatology of Alonso's disease is quickly diagnosed by the good physician: "El pulso de los amantes / es el rostro. Aojado estás." (794-a.) The observation has great significance when it is understood in the light of Fabia's admission that she had already noticed his plight the day before: "Ayer / te vi en la feria perdido / tras una cierta doncella." (794-a.) Love as a sickness, a bewitchment, a fascination, are common metaphors and similes in courtly poetry, and the protagonist's description of his malady is in keeping with the rhetoric of his predecessors. It is not until the end of the first scene, when the dramatist hints darkly that Fabia is no ordinary intermediary, that the ironic complexion of what has been said can be fully appreciated, for it is there that Tello alludes to her franchise with the devil. Thus the final moment reinforces suspicions which are always tangential to *alcahuetería*.

To a modern reader perhaps the most puzzling and disconcerting passage in the dialogue occurs in the middle of the long *relación* in which Alonso recounts how he saw Inés at the fair. He describes an instant of sheer clairvoyance:

> En una capilla entraron
> yo, que siguiéndolas iba,
> entré imaginando bodas.
> ¡Tanto quien ama imagina!
> Vime sentenciado a muerte,
> porque el amor me decía:
> "Mañana mueres, pues hoy
> te meten en la capilla." (795-a)

This is the first in a series of such revelations which Alonso will experience. It must be understood on three levels. The first is related to the nature of his attraction to Inés. It is clear from his dialogue that he is aflame with passion, and passion, as was demonstrated above, is diametrically opposed to marriage. Now, Alonso has summoned Fabia precisely because, for a while at least, his intention is to enjoy the intricacies of a dance of love. With her arrival, then, the *danza* begins. Fabia's part in this affair can hardly be said to lead to marriage. Stated in another way, were Alonso genuinely interested in matrimony at this time, he would not have contracted for the offices of the *tercera*. The truth of this affirmation will become abundantly clear when Rodrigo is introduced. If marriage is the death of passion, then secrecy and absence represent love's source of life. Octavia, of *Los amantes sin amor*, says to Beatriz that love (passion) succumbs "por ausencia o casamiento, / por público sentimiento." (NRAE, III, 157-b.)

Why, then, we might ask, does Alonso tell us that once in the chapel he thought about marriage? The answer is manifestly stated in the Chaplain's treatise: "Even love's commandments warn us not to choose for our love any woman whom we would not properly seek to marry." (*ACL*, 23.) Inés is of the proper station and beauty, thus by the same criterion the courtly decorum would not be violated were she to become the object of Cupid's dart. But even the very thought of marriage, however fleeting, is not in consonance with the relationship that Alonso has in mind with the lady. Thus the vision of his own death at this moment represents the logical consequence of this error. Marriage is contracted in the Church *(la capilla)*, and it is there that the hero is told he will die if his passion happens to find itself some day before the altar. With the chapel emblem, and the world of social convention which it communicates, together with the presence of Fabia, it becomes clear that the protagonist has gone beyond the confines of society's laws and stepped into the lyrical atmosphere of courtly phantasy. The brief experience in the church, therefore, defines the order of etiquette which this leavetaking imposes upon its agents.

The second and third levels of reference on which the clairvoyance rests are rooted in the contemporary understanding of love sickness and the powers of the witch. Young men who had fallen victim to the erotic passion were thought to be legitimately ill with a strange and often deadly kind of physical and spiritual consumption. Excessive passion could eventually disturb the rational faculties and cause the phantasy to supplant reason as the dominant directing agency in the psyche. The inevitable result of such a disorder was that the brain became clouded, the judgement impaired, and the patient was rendered incapable of seeing things as they were. Quevedo says: "Cuando una pasión se apodera del alma, el gusto es cebo del sentido; el sentido queda esclavo del deseo, éste es incendio del corazón, el corazón tiene espíritus muy señores; éstos ofuscan el entendimiento y le hacen idolatrar aquello que es objeto de la pasión." [2] Thus Alonso's prescience is seen also to be the first sign of the dreadful love melancholy which, if allowed to progress unchecked, would lead to certain death. Those unfortunates who were afflicted with the disorder were given to moments of clairvoyance which announced dreadful visions of destruction and self-annihilation. In the "Dedicatoria" to *El desconfiado,* directed to Alfonso Sánchez, Lope says of the phenomenon: "Et confusiones spirituum ascendentium ad cerebrum et caput turbantium..." (RAE, IV, 477.)

Of no less cogency in attempting to assess the effect Alonso's revelation might have had on his public is the popular idea that witches could induce inordinate love in their victims. Sprenger and Krämer call this wickedness "Philocaption":

> Philocaption, or inordinate love of one person for another, can be caused in three ways. Sometimes it is due merely to a lack of control over the eyes; sometimes to the temptation of devils; sometimes to the spells of necromancers and witches, with the help of devils... Incitement to inordinate love by devils through witches... indeed is the best known and most general form of witchcraft. (*Malleus*, 170.)

At this point it is essential to understand that, despite the procuress's feigned ignorance of Alonso's infatuation, she did nevertheless admit that she was present at the village fair when Inés and Alonso first exchanged glances (794-a.), and this fact is of the utmost importance, since Lope has chosen to mention it and thus fix the relationships in time. Such was the horror that those instructed in the black arts could inspire in the Middle Ages and Renaissance that it was held by peasant and scholar alike that the enchanters, with only a glance of their malevolent eyes, could

---

[2] Francisco de Quevedo, "Sentencia 346", in *Obras completas en prosa,* ed. Luis Astrana Marín (Madrid, 1932), 786.

awaken inner turbulence and generate disease. The authors of the *Malleus* explain this action:

> For... the mind of a man may be changed by the influence of another mind. And that influence which is exerted over another often proceeds from the eyes, for in the eyes a certain subtle influence may be concentrated. For the eyes direct their glance upon a certain object without taking notice of other things, and although the vision be perfectly clear, yet at the sight of some impurity, the eyes will as it were contract a certain impurity. This is what Aristotle says in his work *On Sleep and Walking*, and thus if anybody's spirit be inflamed with malice or rage, as is often the case with old women, then their disturbed spirit looks through their eyes, for their countenances are most evil and harmful. (*Malleus*, 17.)

No less an authority than Juan Luis Vives affirms the danger surrounding the *celestinas*:

> Aquella mujer que, pagada por el galán, con palabras blandas solicita y empuja a la maldad, carece de nombre en el diccionario humano, puesto que es una cosa diabólica... No sufra, pues, la doncella ni siquiera su aspecto, que basiliscos son o como los cataplebos de Plinio, con sus agudísimos ojos, infiltran ponzoña y matan no más que con la vista. Y aún hay algunas de esas celestinas de tan satánica habilidad, que muchas veces conquistan con sólo mirar, sin auxilio de razonamiento. Y aún hay otras que se valen de hechizos y encantamientos, de cuyas maneras de proceder ojalá fuesen más raros los ejemplos. Y qué decir si las hay que con el solo saludo, o la sonrisa, o el guiño, a guisa de serpiente, mancha a la doncella a quien miró, especialmente entre aquellos que conocen el arte diabólico de la mujer, por no decir cuánta infección y cuán inextirpable contrae la casa en la que alguna vez pusiere los pies.[3]

That the distressed lovers of courtly lineage often experienced such "revelaciones del alma," as Alonso will later call them, can be abundantly observed in the prose and verse they bequeathed to subsequent generations. Against this background, Alonso's vision

---

[3] Juan Luis Vives, *Formación de la mujer cristiana*, in *Obras completas*, trans. Lorenzo Riber (Madrid, 1947), I, 1026-27.

is in consonance with his kind and with the creed which governed their morality. But even the troubadours were aware of the sickness which love occasioned and regarded it as a natural concomitant of their passion. The "espíritus muy señores," of which Quevedo speaks, became the agent of their peculiar insight into truth. But if the erotic infirmity afflicted Love's followers, how much more lethal was its germ when carried by Lucifer's minions?

Alonso's *representación*, therefore, which he says disturbed him, expresses the confluence of the courtly convention with 'modern science' and contemporary sensitivity to the *alcahueta-bruja* as an agent of perversity. Just as in the vision, so is the entire scene textured to create a reality that is bipartite. Thus from the initial moments of the play, the ambivalent complexion of the action becomes apparent. Because the spectator knows that the hero must die, both dialogue and action assume a double reference throughout. Thus when Fabia says "Aojado estás" (794-a.), or, "a gran peligro te pones" (795-a.), and when the hero refers to the "miracles" she will work (795-b.), the metaphorical and literary is seen to be all too real.

Scene two (iii-ix)

Scene two is divided into four moments: the dialogue between Inés and Leonor, the arrival of Fabia, the entrance of Rodrigo and Fernando, and finally there is a return to the conversation of the two maidens. We enter the discussion *in medias res*. Inés has fallen profoundly in love with the young *galán* whom she saw at the fair. (795-b.) Her surrender to Cupid's arrow, similar to Alonso's capitulation, is total: "Sea ansí." (795-b.) And echoing the protagonist's description of his illness, she discourses on the "ocular agents" of this enrapturing flame. (795-b.) We know forthwith that Fabia's task will not be a difficult one.

The heroine's rather rhetorical question —"¿quién concierta y desconcierta/ este amor y desamor?" (795-b.)— urges the spectator to seek an answer: the solution is not long in presenting itself. The servant announces the arrival of one Fabia, seller of cosmetics which hide the face of *voluptas*. Leonor hesitates to permit entry to one "que no tiene buena fama." (796-a.) It is Inés who both symbolically and literally issues the command that permits admission to Love's emissary. In this, she duplicates Alonso's summons and thus also begins to move from the inner circle of respectability and safety into love's garden. With the heroine's acquiescence, the social dimensions of the play become discernible. Acceptable love has no need of *terceras,* and proper young maidens, as Vives affirms, should flee the presence of old hags peddling pigments of scarlet and purple: "Corra, pues, la doncella a su madre como a un sagrado refugio y cuéntele los manejos de la Celestina; o de tal manera se le ha de esquivar y rechazar, que entienden los que lo vieren, que en ella temes una peste." (Vives, *Mujer cristiana, ed. cit.,* I, 1027.)

This scene is literally studded with Fabia's asides that, together with other dramatic semaphores, boldly reveal the tissue of deception separating appearance from reality.. The game of love which began with Inés disguised as a *labradora* (794-a.) has now become a play in which all the participants act out their parts: Inés feigns ignorance concerning the true nature of the letter; Fabia pretends to be a blessed old dame seeking help on a certain errand; previously Alonso had bemoaned his courtly affliction and would have us believe that only the "santas manos" of Fabia could assuage his pain; and finally, with Rodrigo's entry, Fabia casts herself in the role of a washerwoman come to pick up the laundry. This surface of obvious dissimulation together with the repeated *apartes* powerfully reflects the ironic understructure on which the scene is built. Fabia's wonderful basket, in which are contained "pastillas, polvos, alcanfor, y solimán," is a remarkably adequate symbol of this multilayered dramatic action when considered in the light of Pedro Ciruelo's discussion of *aojamiento.* The sixteenth century savant warns good Christians to beware of those tutored in the evil sciences who can bewitch with physical objects as well as spells: "Haze el demonio aquellos males trayendo invisiblemente cosas ponçoñosas y contrarias a la complexión de aquel a quien quiere dañar que con solo el olor o vapores altera y corrompe los humores: y causa de enfermedad en la carne y en los nervios." [4]

---

[4] Pedro Ciruelo, *Reprobación de las supersticiones y hechizerias. Libro muy utile y necessario a todos los buenos christianos* (s.l., 1547), Parte tercera, capitulo quinto [pagination lacking].

ACT I 93

There can be little doubt that Inés is fully aware of her part in this illicit game and is quite willing to carry it through. The reception she accords to Alonso's message, sent to her by a go-between, stands in sharp contrast to the posture of decorum and "well educated aloofness" with which she greets Rodrigo's arrival: "Mi padre ha venido ya./ Vuesas mercedes se vayan/ o le visiten; que siente/ que nos hablen, aunque calla." (798-a.) The secret affair which Alonso and Fabia have created, most patently, must exclude don Pedro. Rodrigo's entrance at this point into the action functions in such a way as to illuminate the stark irony of this first liaison between Fabia and Inés in that his strategic arrival focuses our attention on the fact that the heroine is keenly aware of the correct social proprieties. "Either speak to my father or leave," she admonishes, in a display of blushing etiquette, having just handed Fabia the reply to Alonso's correspondence. And finally, at the end of the scene, Leonor reproves her sister's *necedades* (798-b.), exhorting her "to flee love when it begins." (799-a.) Inés's reply betrays her understanding of the distinction between socially oriented love and secret passion which is generated in nature itself: "Nadie del primero huye/ porque dicen que le influye,/ la misma naturaleza." (799-a.) Rodrigo's presence, therefore, provides the point of perspective that polarizes the dramatic conception into two dimensions: the public and social as opposed to the private and secret. Symbolically he is the "insider," a resident of Medina, and in all that he does throughout the play, his behavior is accountable within the established canons of social correctness. Alonso, on the other hand, is an "outsider," a citizen of Olmedo, whose consuming passion forces him to leave the public domain, seek out the services of one who dwells on the fringes of respectability, and thus submerge the affair with Inés into forbidden waters, to go "underground," as it were, where the witches revel.

Scene three (x-xi)

This third segment of Act I is divided into two moments of cardinal importance. Fabia has returned to Alonso's quarters. In the way she reconstructs all that happened with Inés we recognize immediately that what she says is false. Like her fifteenth-century predecessor, she complains of how she was abused and beaten by "dos lacayos y tres pajes" (799-a.) in the service of Inés, thus leading Alonso to believe that his attempted *rapprochement* was a decided failure. This is the first time that Lope has allowed us to witness unequivocally an *engaño* of Fabia's making, since we know that the tale she spins is categorically not true. For all of the playfulness with which she addresses her "patient," the dramatic impact of the dialogue resembles that of a cat toying with the mouse before dining. The irony of the discourse is now apparent:

> ALONSO: Ello ha sido disparate
> que yo me atreviese al cielo.
> TELLO: Y que Fabia fuese el ángel
> que al infierno de los palos
> cayese por levantarte. (799-a.)

For Fabia is no angel, nor has she descended into hell *to save* the hero. But, of course, it is Tello who makes the remark rather than Alonso, who is now thoroughly blinded by his passion. So much so, in fact, that he is incapable of comprehending his own realization that the adventure he pursues represents an "atrevimiento al cielo." As soon as Fabia delivers Inés's reply, the hero, like the heroine before him, prefers to forget the transgression his passion bespeaks. Lope carefully coordinates the protagonist's plunge into Fabia's trap with the coming of the night, passion's symbolic medium: "La vecina/ noche, en los últimos fines/ con que va expirando el día,/ pone los helados pies," Alonso remarks (799-b.), and thus prepares to walk into darkness.

Now we hear the full irony of Tello's sarcastic comment. Alonso leaves the stage to Fabia and the servant. If night is the mantle that cloaks passion's conclave, it is no less the friendly veil that conceals the warlock's salute to Satan's lordship. Fabia announces her intention to secure the tooth of a hanged *salteador*. (800-a.) Nowhere in Act I does the ironic design of tragedy manifest itself more clearly as action and counteraction than here when Lope wrenches the mask of Eros from Fabia's face to reveal the devil's mark. This conversation reverberates throughout all the preceding action and will continue to echo in the events to follow. We are allowed to see Fabia as Lucifer's agent in disguise, and thus the hidden danger lying just beneath the action of the play momentarily rises to the surface at exactly the time of the prelude to the first meeting of the lovers. Lope's adjustment of the play to the drama of *maleficium* at this juncture corresponds to his world's conception of Satan's treacherous strategy as Alexo Venegas describes it:

> Mas porque es él [the demon] la suma malicia y la misma desorden, bien se puede creer dél que ni deja vado ni portillo ni piedra que no mueva para turbar al agonista. Para lo cual pues en el infierno no se guarda, como dice Job la orden de la naturaleza, es verisímile que su morador siga la confusión babilónica y confunda las tentaciones y anteponga y posponga y girone y remiende y edifique y destruya y trueque, como dice Horacio, cuadrado con lo redondo, é como orgulloso sofista presuma hacer del cielo cebolla y vuelve en blanco lo negro, como el alguacil de moscas, que con las barbas blancas que muestra de fuera encubre los hábitos negros que tiene de dentro, con que prende las moscas.[5]

Tello's *caveat*, "Quien sube por tales pasos/ Fabia, el mismo fin espera," (800-a.) underscores the ambivalence of the night symbolism, for night, like the "alguacil de moscas," invites the unsuspecting lovers to enjoy its protection with "hábitos negros que prenden las moscas."

Scene four (xii-xiii)

It is fitting that the first abortive meeting of the lovers, then, should be enacted at night. Poetically, the darkness expresses a multiplicity of dramatic and conceptual perspectives. Passion is scarcely an emotion that can be put on public display because of its illicit nature. Night, then, has always been the favorite time for a courtly truancy. But, Love, as Alonso says (793-b.), is a blind god who in turn deprives its subjects of their reason and "sight."

---

[5] Alexo Venegas, *Agonía del tránsito de la muerte con los avisos y consuelos que cerca della son provechosas*, NBAE, XVI, 190-b.

Now, in the darkness the lovers literally cannot see, which fact dramatically and ironically objectifies the courtly disposition of passionate trysts. The nocturnal backdrop of Scene four reflects in miniature the ironic design of the play as a whole, in the sense that true tragedy is precisely the record of man's inability to see, and therefore to understand, the structuring of events which fate has decreed. As the action moves forward Lope will utilize this powerful symbol with increasing effectiveness. The representative lack of vision on the part of all the participants is first articulated by Rodrigo who cannot at this point grasp the tragic potential of his complaints: "...que cuanto más doña Inés/ con sus desdenes me mata,/ tanto más me enciende el pecho." (800-b.) The *cuanto más ... tanto más* device, so characteristic of the fifteenth-century *cancionero* poets, exactly synthesizes both Rodrigo's and Alonso's destiny in the following relationship: the more Inés favors Alonso, the more the fires of jealousy will consume Rodrigo; the more the love affair develops, the less capable are those involved of seeing its direction, and thus the closer they draw to catastrophe. The courtly emotional paradox constitutes the very fiber of the tragic irony.

Even more sightless than Rodrigo is Alonso. Speaking *en gracioso*, Tello informs his master that he must assist the old bawd to "sacar una dama de su casa," (801-a.) a matter of "grandísima importancia" to Fabia (800-b.), which is, of course, the same purpose behind Alonso's nocturnal visit. The protagonist warns his man: "no entres a donde no salgas." (801-a.) Yet when Tello directly explains the nature of his mission (801-a.), Alonso appears not to have heard a word, since his next remark has nothing to do with Tello's confession. The hero looks but cannot see, he listens but cannot hear. It is likewise in the shadows that the confusion about the ribbon takes place, and this mixup is soon to become the immediate complicating factor which sets the action on its tragic course. Neither *galán* should have been there: Rodrigo, because Inés had made clear her disdain toward him; Alonso, because of the moral violation his passion represents. Both are smitten with passion, and in the symbolic darkness of night the fatal error is committed because neither can 'see.'

At this all-important moment in Act I, Lope's morphology of scenes is the factor that conditions the spectator's histrionic experience. The last segment of action seen just prior to this confusion explicitly communicates Fabia's sinister identity. Likewise the dramatist interposes her image through Tello's dialogue in such a way that a metaphorical parallel is established relating the purpose of Alonso's presence —literally to bring his lady love out of her house— with Fabia's nocturnal activity—figuratively "para sacar una dama de su casa." (801-a.) Indeed, at the very moment in which Alonso awaits the appearance of Inés, Tello informs us that he is already overdue for his engagement. One can suppose, therefore, that the secret rendezvous occurs at about the same time that Fabia is busy at the execution platform. Thus before, during and throughout what occurs on stage, the shadow of one who is "enseñada a hablar al diablo" (800-a.) permeates the darkness. The dramatic innuendo that behind it all are the witch's *conjuros* is further set forth in Scene five, when Rodrigo arrives at don Pedro's house with the ribbon in his possession. Leonor is the first to exclaim: "Fabia este engaño te ha hecho." (802-a.) Inés then comments: "Todo fué enredo de Fabia." (802-a.) And finally the heroine again expostulates: "Oh Fabia embustera!" (802-b.) What may be sheer surmise on their part—that is, that in some way Fabia has brought about this calamity—to the spectator, having witnessed more of the action, begins to assume a relationship of cause and effect; or so it would have seemed to the *mosquetero* who firmly believed, like Venegas and Pope Innocent's inquisitors, that Hell's order was not that of this earth and that the demon, through his agents, could manipulate the disposition of things in nature to effect evil purposes. The *Malleus* affirms:

> This then is our proposition: devils by their art do bring about evil effects through witchraft, yet it is true that without the assistance of some agent they cannot make any form, either substantial or accidental, and we do not maintain that they can inflict damage without the assistance of some agent, but with such an agent diseases, and other human passions or ailments, can be brought about, and these are real and true. (*Malleus*, 11.)

Scene five (xiv-xvii)

The Act draws to a close with a final synthesis of perspectives. Rodrigo, the insider, now materially in possession of the green ribbon, directs himself, as he should, to don Pedro to ask for his daughter's hand in marriage. The contrast between the two *galanes* is set forth in bold relief. Rodrigo's comportment represents the very center of decorous propriety, and Alonso's, the mandate of *cortesía*. Both Inés and her *señor* have now definitely taken the decisive step into the world of passion's protocol. Interestingly, the line separating the lovers from Rodrigo's posture is clearly indicated in the physical position of the actors on stage. On one side we see Rodrigo conversing with Pedro about the possibility of matrimony: on the other huddled together in utter astonishment, Leonor and Inés, Alonso, of course, being absent; two groups, two distinct approaches to love, now set tragically one against the other as protagonist and antagonist.

Christian union, with the considerations it occasions, is the focal point of this scene. It is logical that the Act should end with this central issue, for Lope makes it clear that there is no concrete reason why Alonso could not have asked for Inés. Pedro's only criterion for his daughter's marriage is that she be in love with the suitor. From Rodrigo's request he infers: "Habréle Inés concertado/ con la llave del favor." (802-a.) And a moment later we learn that he wants his future son-in-law to love his daughter in return. (802-a.) Why, then, does Alonso not proceed like Rodrigo? The answer originates in the peculiar logic of courtly passion. Lope's inclusion of an antagonist to indicate the dichotomy between social and natural philosophies establishes a clarity which is relatively lacking in the *Celestina* where there is no counter-suitor to Calisto. The organization of social dimensions in Lope's play is the stone on which the dramatist rests the tragic edifice. Doristo's words are pertinent at this point: "Es amor una pelea/ de la razón y el sentido,/ y un peligro conocido/ que se busca y se desea." (*Los muertos vivos*, NRAE, VII, 645-a.) A degree of danger is essential for the courtly excursion, and this knowledge, in part, explains why the devout of Eros consciously place themselves a good distance from the axis of safety. But it is in the focus of the danger that the irony of this violation becomes evident. To the hero, the risk presents itself merely as a possibility of losing the bid. Similarly, Inés is aware only of a danger to her reputation. (796-a and 802-b.) But in moving beyond the social periphery, there exists the high probability that the adventurer will fall in with those who reside outside not for their truancies, but rather because of their *maleficium*. Since courtesy's faithful cannot see in their land of blissful darkness, by the same token they have no way of recognizing that their dance partner may be Charon rather than Venus. Both Diego de San Pedro and Iñigo de Mendoza, more experienced than Alonso and Inés in the ways of *cortesía*, admonish caution above all. Don Diego says: E lo que más deue proueer, es que... no yerre con priessa... que le hará passar muchas vezes por donde no cumple, a buscar mensajeros que no le conuienen." [6] Alonso would have been well advised to heed Fray Iñigo's warning: "Mas affirmo ser herror/ (perdonen si bien non fablo)/ en su obra el trobador/ inuocar al dios de amor/ para seruicio del diablo." [7]

With these thoughts in mind, the dramatic rationale for locating the conversation between Fabia and Tello immediately prior to the first tryst is of vital concern to the development of tragic probability. Once we know that Fabia's wonderful basket contains a lock of the devil's hair, we are eminently prepared for the likelihood of the fatal accident that follows in the darkness of the night. What the innocent protagonists see merely as possible danger now takes on the scent of probable peril. And because of the psychology of feeling and intuition that Lope has worked into his play, we now suspect that Rodrigo's presence at the *reja*, despite Fernando's comment on the futility of it all (800-a.), falls within the purview of the go-between's gran design. Lope leaves us with a final aside that confirms such a sinister presentiment:

> INÉS: Que siendo ansí, los que fueron
> a la reja le tomaron,
> y por favor se le han puesto.
> De suerte estoy, madre mía,
> que no puedo hallar sosiego
> si no es pensando en quien sabes.
> FABIA (Ap.): (¡Oh, qué bravo efecto hicieron
> los hechizos y conjuros!
> La victoria me prometo.) (802-b.)

Fabia's *aparte*, then, relates gallows to *reja*, and action to play. Thus by the end of the first Act the tension of anticipation which accompanies the inevitable has impregnated the spectacle.

---

[6] Diego de San Pedro, *Sermón de amor*, in M. Menéndez y Pelayo, *Orígenes de la novela*, NBAE, VII, 37-b.
[7] Iñigo de Mendoza, "Vita Christi," in *CC*, I, 2.

ACT II

The morphology of Act II can be divided into five major scenes as follows: Scene one, Alonso, Tello, Pedro, Inés; Scene two, Fernando, Rodrigo; Scene three, the "charade scene," Inés, Tello, Fabia, Leonor, Pedro; Scene four, el Rey Juan II, Álvaro de Luna; Scene five, Alonso, Tello. Fundamentally, the entire Act is constructed on two principal dramatic moments: Scenes one and two, and the remaining three scenes.

Scene one (i-v)

Lope begins the Act with a disquieting mixture of gaiety and brooding. On the one hand, we see the hero now firmly committed to a courtly posture. The promise of a passionate adventure has fully possessed the young man's soul causing him to express his state of mind in the poetic figures characteristic of the *cancioneros*. Like the lovesick elite of an earlier day, Alonso's head is filled with the image of Inés. His attitude can only be described as a histrionic transcription of courtesy's joyous lyricism. Tello, on the other hand, can hardly be said to share his master's exuberance. It should be pointed out here that throughout the course of the drama both the servant and Leonor function as spokesmen for the world of trite-but-safe common sense and objectivity which the hero and heroine have left behind. Thus, Leonor and the *gracioso* can see, hear, and understand what the youthful protagonists can no longer recognize. The servant's disturbing apprehensions counterposed with Alonso's sightless abandon create a somewhat *claroscuro* dramatic atmosphere.

ACT II   101

Since the end of Act I, two factors, which have greatly disturbed Tello, have entered into the course of events. He informs his master that Rodrigo must surely know of the affair. (804-a.) His indiscretion was in having been seen wearing the antagonist's cape lost during the scuffling at Inés's *reja*. To the lackey's unclouded mind, the very presence of Rodrigo can only signify great danger: "Advierte, señor, por Dios,/ que toda esta gente es grave,/ y que están en su lugar,/ donde todo gallo canta." (804-a.) Moreover, he can see no good in a love which begins "por tantas hechicerías, cercos, y conjuros." (804-a.) Thus, through Tello's misgivings, Lope again returns to Fabia's necromancy which was left partially suspended in Act I in the sense that we never found out precisely what she did during, and immediately after, the first abortive meeting of the lovers. Tello recounts in terrifying detail how the corpse spoke to him as Fabia climbed up to the gallows to pry loose a tooth. (804-a.) The inclusion of this *relación* within the line dedicated to Tello's extended admonition deserves a careful scrutiny.

Lope adjusted the *reja* scene in Act I to coincide roughly in time sequence with Fabia's diabolical activities. But it should also be borne in mind that Tello was with Alonso during the entire episode. We must conclude, therefore, that the experience of the *gracioso* with the *tercera* occurred after he left his master and, consequently, posterior to the incident with Rodrigo. Would it not have been more effective for both actions to have taken place simultaneously rather than within an approximate time interval? The answer must be sought in the histrionic effect which Tello's presence at the *reja* produces. Although both events may not have come about concurrently, the inclusion of Tello in the hero's first rendezvous provides the dramatist with another opportunity to insinuate Fabia's silhouette into the spectacle, thus creating the *impression* of a synchronous action, since she was as busy as Alonso and Rodrigo. At the beginning of Act II, Lope once again projects Fabia's ectoplasm onto the stage, thereby resolving the suspension which had been deliberately worked into the final moments of the first *jornada*. Despite the mood of joy emanating from Alonso, we are permitted a nightmarish glimpse of the concealed *maleficium*. More important still is the way in which Lope introduces the ghoulish disclosure. The previous twenty-five lines of discourse refer to Rodrigo's suspicions, followed immediately by the twenty-one lines devoted to the *relación*. The common denominator, therefore, in Tello's warnings is the danger he sees from both outside the love affair (Rodrigo), and from within (Fabia's *conjuros*). We are thus led from Rodrigo to Fabia in one uninterrupted flow of speech *as if* there were a causal relationship between the activities of these two characters, although it cannot be said that in Tello's mind there exists such a clearly defined induction. We hear both admonitions, nevertheless, in the same frame of reference: peril.

The servant's deeply felt uneasiness about Rodrigo's possible reaction to Alonso might well be envisioned as little more than the natural hesitation of an outsider contemplating the course of *loco amor*, were it not for the existence of Scene two, in which the anti-hero makes us fully aware of his suspicions and growing displeasure over the mystrious competitor. We shall consider this action sequence with Rodrigo and Fernando as logically conjunctive to Scene one, although it is an independent unit in both time and space. Its position relative to the development of the stage action powerfully orients the spectator's mode of experiencing the courtly nature of the hero's initial appearance. Essentially, Scene two reinforces the atmosphere of somber adumbration conveyed through the servant's disquieting premonitions. Thus the love duet which occupies most of Scene one has as its overture Tello's *caveat* and as its coda the scene with Rodrigo and his companion. Morphologically, therefore, the meeting is virtually encased in dialogue sequences that create a sense of imminent catastrophe. What Tello suspected in the opening moments is now dramatically confirmed as we see Rodrigo's jealousy turn to murderous hatred of his antagonist. Rodrigo, the socially oriented man, like Tello and Leonor, regards the secret affair as *deshonesto,* calling for the death of Alonso: "Yo he de matar a quien vivir me cuesta/ en su desgracia, porque tanto olvido/ no puede proceder de honesto intento." (808-b.) His full designation as an antagonist represents the dramatic materialization of the courtly pattern which requires an impediment to passionate love, and, because of such an obstacle, an area of recognizable danger constituting the backdrop against which the traditional forms of *fin amor* can be played out.

Scenes one and two, then, achieve an orchestration of the tragic reality by differentiating character participations which, in turn, identify the various simultaneities of action. Rodrigo's role defines the counterforce within the game of love enacted through Alonso and Inés and expressed dramatically as a play. Lope thus accommodates the courtly design that demands a perilous *milieu* to this plot disposition. The dramatist has, moreover, skillfully revealed the presence of still another histrionic perspective, that having to do with Fabia's sorcery. It is Tello's narration of the tooth episode expressed jointly with his anxiety about Rodrigo that prompts the spectator to begin experiencing the Alonso-Inés-Rodrigo triangle as subordinate to a far more comprehensive plan related to Fabia's *hechizos*. Lope thus states his tragic ambivalence as two action quantities: a play with its counterplay set against a drama of diabolical intervention.

We return to the night darkness for the dramatic atmosphere in which the first real contact between the two lovers takes place. If a courtly posture was formulated in Act I, the beginning of Act II portrays Alonso and his lady as marionettes dancing to the stylized forms of love's melody. Lope's scene is a perfect reproduction of the poetic protocol reminiscent of the *cancioneros*. Absence from the beloved is an agony comparable only to death itself: "Tengo el morir por mejor,/Tello, que vivir sin ver," Alonso remarks in the first two lines of the Act. The lover swears eternal fealty to his lady, "porque Inés mi dueña es/ para vivir o morir." (804-b.) While aware of the danger inherent in secret love, Alonso replies to Tello's apprehensions, that true love can never concern itself with the threat of discovery or reprisal: "Tello, un verdadero amor/ en ningún peligro advierte." (804-a.) Love's flame provides life and death at the same time, Inés affirms: "...pues de una suerte/ me da vida y me da muerte." (805-a.) Living as a perpetual dying for the sake of the beloved is the theme of the poem which Alonso has composed for Inés: "...dile cuál me ves/ por ella muriendo; Dile, Andrés, que ya me veo/ muerto por volverla a ver." (806-a.) The very glance of the lady's eyes, the poem continues, revives the moribund lover sufficiently to begin his death agonies anew: "Verdad es que se dilata,/ el morir, pues con mirar/ vuelve a dar vida la ingrata,/ y así se cansa en matar,/ pues da vida a cuantos mata." (806-a.) The gloss depicts the lady as a kind of *belle dame sans merci:* "...dile a mi hermosa homicida/ que por qué se mata en mí,/ pues que sabe que es mi vida." (806-a.) Longing to be near is a living death: "...que me habrá muerto el deseo." (806-a.) The greatest of all *galardones* is, nevertheless, to live dying for the love of such a distant *señora:* "...que no hay bien como vivir/ por ella muriendo." (806-a.) Thus, not only do the protagonists act out the forms of the courtly pattern, but also speak to one another in the peculiar idiom of the troubadours.

Alonso and Inés play the game of love "by the rules," as it were, totally unaware that their delicious interlude is really an enactment of a most real truth, a veritable dance of death, a literalization of the literary. For love is blind, as Miguel Sabuco de Nantes admonishes, an emotional suspension of reason that clouds the understanding, making everything ruled by passion appear to be other than it really is:

> Síguese ahora el efecto del amor y el deseo. El amor ciega, convierte al amante en la cosa amada, lo feo hace hermoso y lo falso perfecto, todo lo allana y pone igual; lo dificultoso hace fácil, alivia todo trabajo, da salud cuando lo amado se goza. También mata en dos maneras: o perdiendo lo que se ama, o no pudiendo alcanzar lo que se ama y desea.[1]

In such a *mundo al revés* it is not surprising that Alonso sees Rodrigo and Fabia as mere stage props, parts of a dramatic setting, the ultimate goal of which is the attainment of ecstasy. In this state of narcosis, flowers are stars, valleys are heavens: "...después que las bellas/ plantas de Inés goza el valle,/tanto florece con ellas,/ que quiso el cielo trocalle/ por sus flores sus estrellas./ Ya el valle es cielo, después/ que su primavera es,/ pues verá el cielo en el suelo/ quien vió, pues Inés es cielo." (805-b.) And the lady, of course, is the sun itself. (808-a.) Thus, entry into the tabernacle of Venus brought with it a strange new condition of life in which the votaries' understanding is paralyzed by the sweet venom of Love's dart. They move, as if in a trance, through a hall of mirrors which are all turned toward the lovers in such a way that they can see only their own beautiful image.

---

[1] In Florencio M. Torner, *Doña Oliva Sabuco de Nantes Siglo XVI* (Madrid, 1935), 101.

The center of this first dramatic segment of Act II is Alonso's love poem spoken by Tello. As the *gracioso* recites his master's verses to Inés, the spectator passes from a simple witness to an interpreter. Such a subtle conversion is brought about by three factors. First is his foreknowledge of the hero's impending demise. Alonso's poetic offering, therefore, heavy with the life-death polarity, is immediately referred to this prior acquaintance with the legend, and hence translated into the ambivalent idiom of high tragedy. The poem's dramatic environment itself further suggests that love and death are implicated in the activities of Fabia and Rodrigo. The plot disposition, then, adds to the ironic interweave of Tello's recital to Inés. Finally, the poem must be heard against the contemporary social understanding of passion which held that such a love interposed a veil of illusion between its victims and the world in which they lived. The dream-like phantasy which its devotees describe so poetically is regarded by Vives as little more than an "atroz veneno" which most probably will lead to death:

> Pues es de saber que el amor, por dominar y ampliar más y más su señorío en nuestra alma, y perturbarlo todo, y revolverlo, y mezclarlo por arriba y por abajo, lo primero que hace es cegar el entendimiento o desalojarle, a fin de que cuando no vea nada o esté muy lejos, no pueda conocer lo que pasa en su misma casa y se le permita libremente el capricho del amor, trastornarla y revolucionarla. Atroz veneno éste, que nos priva de la vista y cuando nos tiene ciegos nos arrastra por mil barrancos y por otros tantos precipicios, y las más de las veces nos hace rodar a un sumidero, donde hallamos la muerte. (*Mujer cristiana,* ed. cit., I, 1051-a.)

What is of interest in Vives's diatribe is the unique manner in which the love-afflicted are prone to restructure reality into a new order of lunacy. And aside from the violation of morality about which Vives thunders, Lope's *mosqueteros* were also well aware that the kind of love affair the *Fénix* had set before them might well be due to a sinister meditation, as Tello hinted at the beginning of the Act. According to the *Malleus,* devils, through the witch, could induce inordinate love by darkening the intellect and subverting the reason: "So also the intellect can be darkened by a bad angel in the knowledge of what appears to be true: and this through a confusion of ideas and images received and stored by the perceptions, from which comes an inordinate love of the apparently good, such as bodily delectations, which men seek after." (*Malleus,* 53.) Thus blind passion (Alonso's poem) and uncommon hate (Rodrigo's fulminations) make their appearance simultaneously on stage, both of which the *Malleus* declares, are sure signs of witchery. (*Malleus,* 14.)

Scene three (vii-xi)

Scene three is one of those technically perfect marvels that occur with utmost rarity in the theater. Here the multiple conceptual perspectives of the tragedy are brought together and coordinated in such a way that the ironic vision achieves full realization. If there are any doubts remaining in the spectator's mind concerning the validity of his *double entendre,* Scene three is intended to testify to the correctness of that act of *agudeza.* The genesis of the "charade" is embedded in a remark Alonso directs to his lady: "Aunque fuerza de obediencia / te hiciese tomar estado..." (805-a.) Here, as throughout the drama, the passage from manner of expression to theatrical reality can be observed since this scene dramatizes precisely Inés's pose as a novice.

As love was a game that imposed a set of masking forms on those who played it, so Scene three represents Lope's accommodation of the world of topsy-turvy appearances to a dramatic artifice. The narcotic transformation, of which Sabuco de Nantes and Vives speak, not to mention the *trovadores* themselves, materializes in Lope's tragedy as a masque in which the characters attire themselves in garments that visually symbolize the obvious fact that each is playing a role. We are witness to a moment of delightful, if ironic, play acting intended to reflect the abnormal order of courtesy's mystique. The effect of the charade, however, does more than objectify love's dementia. The masquerade spectacle admirably expresses the background of the social commonplace belief that passionate love was a poison with the savor of honey. Rosela, of ***Don Juan de Castro,*** aptly describes love as "un áspid en hierba, / y un veneno en vaso de oro; / sé que es un traidor leal, / y en el favor y el desdén / *un mal disfrazado bien,* / *y un bien disfrazado mal.*" (RAE, XIV, 51, italics mine.) Rosela's analysis pierces to the very center of the scene's artistry and uncovers the secret of its irony. In the disguises and feigned identities of the masque there is an inherent reminder of the evil design that lurks beneath the face of piety (Rosela's "veneno en vaso de oro," and "áspid en hierba") which characterized the visitations of *alcahuetas* to *casas honestas*. Luis de León warns young ladies of this danger: "Porque debajo de nombre de pobreza, y cubriéndose con piedad, a las veces entran en las casas algunas personas arrugadas y canas, que roban la vida y entiznan la honra, y dañan a el alma de los que viven en ellas y los corrompen sin sentir, los empozoñan, pareciendo que los lamen y halagan."[2] The same writer points out that evil, to achieve its diabolical ends, will attire itself in the clothing and appearances of good, and even "take on its color": "Y aun también acontece, que de la virtud y del vicio, nazcan frutos muy semejantes. Tanto es disimulado el mal, o tanto procura disimularse para nuestro daño... que... para poder vivir y valer, se le [virtue] allega y se viste de él, y desea tomar su color." (*Perfecta casada, ed. cit.,* 281.) The metaphorical and physical *disfraz* associated with love, *alcahuetería,* and evil is no less a commonplace in the parlance of the age when witchcraft is mentioned, for the malefactors too stood in need of a disguise, the better to carry out the devil's commands. Pedro Ciruelo's comments on the saintly aliases of witches will serve to synthesize the foregoing remarks:

> Esta arte [witchcraft] ordena el diablo para tener mucha plática con los hombres, porque por oír las razones que dice el nigromántico y cómo le responde el diablo, allégase mucha gente a los oír; y esto desea mucho el diablo, tener grande auditorio, para con sus razones sembrar algunos errores contra la ley, contra la religión cristiana, y para mandar que hagan algunas obras vanas y supersticiosas só color de santas y devotas. (*Reprobación,* tercera parte, capítulo octavo [pagination lacking].)

---

[2] Luis de León, *La perfecta casada,* in *Obras completas castellanas,* ed. P. Félix García, O. S. A. (Madrid, 1951), 283.

The poetic and dramatic symbolism common to the moral, literary, and social background, integrated through the reality of the tragedy, expresses itself naturally as a mask, a disguise, an imposture. Accordingly, Fabia's pose as a nun, Tello's impersonation of a *magister,* and the heroine's pretense of a religious avocation represent Lope's creative synthesis of mutually conversant traditions. The remarkably rich histrionic ambivalence produced by this concoction is first manifested in the previous love duet. Inés has informed Pedro of a long dormant yearning to become a nun. Tello is quick to see the implementation of Inés's stalling device: he will pass himself off as a Latin teacher, "Y verás con qué destreza / le enseño a leer tus cartas." (807-b.) As for Fabia's role, he says, "Y aún pienso que podrá Fabia / servirte en forma de dueña, / siendo la santa mujer / que con su falsa apariencia / venga a enseñarla." (807-b.) The irony of the whole charade is brilliantly anticipated when Inés replies, "Fabia, será mi maestra / de virtudes y costumbres," (807-b.) and the *gracioso* remarks, "Y ¡qué tales serán ellas!" (807-b.) The delicious duplicity of the dialogue in combination with the fabric of impersonation create a luminescence that spotlights the dual reality of the masquerade.

Scene three demands, then, that the spectacle of the masque be referred to the mysterious and somber inner drama. The ironic order which this coordination of perspectives imposes upon the stage representation materializes immediately with Fabia's entry. The high priestess of Love's cult is disguised as an abbess with rosary, distaff and all. The religious habit synchronizes at once the multiple levels of meaningfulness of which the irony is compounded. It deceives Pedro, and this is, of course, the surface purpose for the *disfraz.* But the *medianera* would have her 'children' believe she is the earthly Pontifex of the religion of *Nuestro Señor don Amor, el Redentor* of all the courtly devout. Now she appears literally dressed as a nun: the metaphorical is made symbolically incarnate. The Christian imposture and garb are delightfully comical in that everyone knows the real identity of the *santa madre.* But the same attire becomes blasphemously ironic when we remember that Fabia is a witch, Satan's adjutant, who is in the act of consecrating the host to the greater glory of her deity, serving, therefore as his priestess "so color de santa y devota," as Ciruelo expresses it.

The three points of view represented on stage in this scene etch out the pattern of irony in which are elaborated, experienced, and recapitulated the various levels of action that form the structural framework of the tragedy. Three exclusive areas of vision are circumscribed by this organization: Pedro sees reality as it appears; Inés, Leonor, Tello, and Fabia know that the forms disguise another substance; Fabia and the audience understand all that happens as expressions of a powerful tragic undertow. The double and often triple strata of meaning that the characters and spectators alike perceive in the dialogue overlay the spectacle on the stage with a striking ironic filigree that is perfectly adjusted to the various angles of vision appropriate to each participant. The following study of some of the lines will demonstrate the interrelationship of discourse to dramatic structure and conception. Fabia's opening remark, "¡Paz sea en esta casa," has three points of reference: *Paz*, i.e. peace in the Christian sense; comfort and solace to the truant lovers; conversely equivocal because 'peace' is not really among the pretty baubles she carries in her basket. "¿Quién es aquella que ya / tiene su Esposo elegido, / y como prenda querida / estos impulsos le da?"; *esposo*, Jesus and Alonso. "...y ella vea / el dueño que vos no véis..." (809-a.); *dueño*, Alonso, Christ. "Aunque en el Señor [Jesus, Alonso, Satan] espero / que os ha de obligar piadoso / a que acetéis tal esposo, / que es muy noble caballero." (809-a.) "Sabiendo que anda a buscar / quien venga a morigerar / los verdes años de Inés, / quien la guíe, quien la muestre / las sémitas del Señor, / [Alonso, don Amor, Jesus, Satan] y al camino del amor, / [Eros, *caritas*] como a principiante adiestre, / hice oración en verdad, / [prayer, tooth extraction] y tal impulso me dió, / que vengo a ofrecerme yo / para esta necesidad, / aunque soy gran pecadora." [Christian humility, *alcahuetería, brujería*] And Pedro replies: "Esta es la mujer, Inés, / que has menester" (809-b.), an irony which Inés underscores when she says, "Esta es / la que he *menester agora*." (809-b, italics mine.) When Pedro further comments, "No he visto humildad igual" (809-b.), the equivocal irony of the Catholic and courtly traditions becomes strikingly apparent. Humility is at once the first of the theological virtues and the fundamental premise of Love's religion. What appears to Pedro to be instruction in the ways of Catholic virtue is actually a ritual initiation into the rites of courtesy's *chaste eloignement*. Thus the dramatist adapts the Catholic format to the needs of the courtly heresy. In the midst of all this artful ambivalence Lope takes great care to remind the audience that behind the charade-farce and beneath the courtly game is the shadowy world of Fabia's forbidden science. In the same way that the spectator's *ingenio* has been trained by now to respond to the irony resulting from ambiguous equivocation, Fabia's remark, "en vano, infernal dragón / la pensabas devorar" (809-b.), will be understood as an ironic *engaño con la verdad* in that her words also contain a double meaning hidden in hypocrisy. Tello's entrance further directs our attention to the many layers of reality that the discourse conveys. "El maestro que buscáis / está aquí, señor don Pedro, / para latín y otras cosas, / que dirá después su efecto" (809-b.), he says. The servant's answer, "Sí señor, de vísperas" (810-a.), to Pedro's inquiry concerning his academic and religious credentials is a clearly ironic reference to Fabia's true identity.

The essential distinction which the baroque *comedia* makes between plot and action, play and drama, is vigorously articulated in the technique of the charade. Nowhere in his tragedy does Lope indicate so lucidly as here that appearance and reality are ironic exponents of one another. In this sense, Scene three serves as a recapitulation of the complex blueprint of the stage spectacle. As the lovers took refuge in the stylized forms of the courtly dance, they now conceal this love in the outward forms of Christian piety so as to prolong the game of passion. The effect of such a dramatic clarification of perspectives is to invite the audience to witness what it sees on stage as an ironic interplay of truth and fiction in which fiction mirrors the cold image of truth. This bold illumination is attained because all that has hitherto been understated, hinted, suggested, is now synthesized in the brilliant overstatement which the scene represents. In the hierarchy of actions, farce, play, drama, the eye of *entendimiento* is focused successively inward toward the very center of the ironic directive that reduces plurality to unity. It should be pointed out that the remarkable structure Lope has given to his re-creation of the legend of the Knight from Olmedo accommodates the inner

ACT II   111

and outer dimensions inherent in the courtly posture as defined so succinctly by Fray Iñigo de Mendoza:

> Como muchas nuezes navas
> se cubren de casco sano,
> como engañosas maçanas
> que muestran color de sanas
> y tienen dentro gusano,
> assy por nuestro dolor,
> muchos de nuestras Españas
> se dan christiana color
> que de dentro el dios de amor
> ha roydo las entrañas. (*CC*, I, 46.)

Scene four (xii)

Scene four represents an interruption in the continuity of the stage action in that two minor personages are introduced discussing a matter totally unrelated to the love affair. In both this and the final moment of Act II, the dramatist prepares for the liaison with the last *jornada*. King John the Second and his Constable, Alvaro de Luna, enter discussing affairs of state. The substance of their conversation has to do with articles of clothing.[3] The Pope has approved a change in the habit of the Knights of the Order of Alcántara. The second matter of urgency also has to do with costume. John wants all Jews and Moslems henceforth to wear articles of clothing that readily identify the bearer as outsiders, that is, not of the Faith, lest the Semites pollute the Gentiles: "Tenga el cristiano el decoro / que es justo: apártese dél; / que con esto tendrán miedo / los que su nobleza infaman." (811-a.) The contrast is made very clear: those who defend the Faith should be more recognizable (the Knights of Alcántara), and those who are enemies likewise must be so marked. With a final word about Alonso, the scene ends.

To those familiar with the techniques of the *comedia*, this short hiatus will be seen as a pause that establishes a parallel between the national and local-personal levels of the tragedy. For

---

[3] For an illuminating discussion of attire as a motif in the tragedy, see C. A. Soons, *art. cit.*

a brief interlude our attention is directed away from the mainstream of action toward the preoccupations of the realm. What is Lope's aesthetic rationale for this abrupt intrusion into an otherwise linear progression? The dramatic function of the break is to reinforce and solidify the ironic reality that the preceding masque sets forth. Unlike the classical style or rationalist view that relates quantities in a rigorous dialectic of cause and result, baroque unity is realized through analogy, and thus relies on the spectator's innate propensity to associate similar forms, designs, or occurences. What the artist hopes to achieve is a oneness of feeling that coordinates independent impressions by emphasizing common forms. Scene four, when understood within the *modus operandi* of the *comedia,* reflects the same irony that emanated from the masquerade itself. The image of John and Alvaro on stage could not fail to remind the spectator of the strange and unnatural domination which the Constable reputedly exerted over the mind of the monarch. This is the reign during which Lope has chosen to place his action, a period characterized by the same phenomenon of will control that the witches were thought to practice on their victims. John's preoccupation with the outer forms of recognition and designation becomes ironic when we recall that the greatest danger to the kingdom was none other than Alvaro himself, as subsequent events demonstrated. Had the King been more inclined to listen to his other advisers, perhaps the affairs of Castile might have developed with greater harmony. But John is as blind to the insidious danger hidden in his inordinate love for the court favorite as Alonso and Inés are to the perils that attend association with *alcahuetas.* The same complexion which defined John's reign, therefore, is mirrored in the daily events of his subjects, or so it would seem from Lope's inclusion of this scene. The seventeenth century view of the fifteenth — an era of *magos,* intrigues, courtly poets, and sorcerers — thus made Alvaro's age a singularly appropriate one for the kind of action that constitutes the *Caballero de Olmedo.* What could have been more likely than for a Fabia to live and practice her forbidden arts during a time contemporaneous with such notables as the Constable or Enrique de Villena? However short Scene four may be, its conceptual sympathy with the rest of the tragedy is unmistakable. As we already know the dolorous resolution of the legend, the impression is created of an inexorable movement toward human sacrifice. The temper of the times would appear to augur grievous and unfortunate events ahead.

Scene five (xiii-xiv)

There is perhaps no play in the Spanish Golden Age that is quite so puzzling as *El Caballero de Olmedo*. How are we to understand the brief moment of clairvoyance experienced by the protagonist in Act I? His painful dream at the end of Act II? The appearance of the ghost and *labrador* in Act III? And most important of all, how do these baffling events relate to the tragic resolution of the legend and the fundamental structure of the play? The answers to these questions must be sought partially in a seventeenth century explanation of the peculiar psychological disturbances the hero undergoes, of which the terrifying dream of Scene five is a major instance. The problem for the modern student is first to comprehend what the dream symbolizes and why it is that the hero's sleep has been troubled of late.

The literature, both poetry and prose, which the medieval troubadours bequeathed to civilization is above all a distinctive blend of poetic delicacy and psychological exploration of the human mind in either distress or ecstatic joy. The courtly songsters seem never to tire of examining the most inaccessible areas of the soul. Their production was, after all, intended to be lyrical, and the lyrical, by definition, is subjective and private, demanding that the poet make objective and public his many complex states of feeling. Courtly poetry, for all its stylization, represents an emotional journal, a diary of the spirit. In short, it has an inherently psychological basis because love, it was believed, was a powerful transforming force that affected the entire human constitution and condition, both physical and emotional. Poetry and ancient medical-psychological theory joined hands to form a unique convention from which all subsequent courtly expression drew its matter until well into the eighteenth century. In the discussion which follows, therefore, we shall attempt to analyze Alonso's dream within the precepts of human understanding germane to the world outlook of his time.

Lope, like his audiences and his medieval predecessors, inherited a theory of the personality from the scientists of Antiquity, notably Aristotle, Hippocrates, and Galen. The body, soul, and mind of every individual represented a specific balance of four humors, plus animal and vital spirits. Blood, the first of the humors, was hot and humid; choler, the second, hot and dry; phlegm, the third, cold and humid; and melancholy, the last, cold and dry. Thus each humor was assigned two corresponding qualities. Ideally, perfect health corresponded to a condition in which the four humors were present in the body in equal amounts. But in reality it was recognized that one humor would predominate over the others, thus determining the personality type of any given man. Moreover, certain humors tended to be more active during the various stages of life. Childhood was a time governed by blood; youth, blood and choler; old age, phlegm; and senility, by melancholy. Infancy and childhood were, therefore, primarily hot and humid, youth, hot and dry, etc. Jerónimo Cortés points out that youth is further subdivided into two classes: adolescence, from 14 to 25, which is hot and dry, and youth, from 25 to 35, the only age span in which the body is *templado*.[4] When a humor appropriate to an age class was more abundant than the others, the organism was held to be in balance and, therefore, in good health. The danger was that one humor might totally dominate the others, thus throwing the delicate alignment into imbalance. When this occurred the body was said to be distempered, and stringent measures were urgently prescribed to re-establish the proper humoral proportions and distributions.

In general it was agreed that the hot and humid qualities were less conducive to a sound organism than the cold and dry ones although, in any case, an excess of one or the other temperature was prejudicial. The melancholy man, therefore, did enjoy the advantage of keen intelligence and remarkable perspicacity because his bodily constitution was cool and dry, the attributes most suitable to intellectual activity. Young men, in whom the hot humors prevailed, naturally were more prone to sudden disorders of the spirit, and, therefore, more likely to fall into humoral

---

[4] Jerónimo Cortés, *Lunario nuevo perpetuo y general y pronostica de los tiempos universales* (Madrid, 1598), 12v.

congestions resulting from an excess of heat. Emotions, like the humors and the elements of nature, were also assigned a place on the temperature spectrum. Love and joy, of all the passions, were the most hot and moist respectively. Now youth, being hot in conjunction with a greater or lesser degree of dryness or moisture because of age, humoral composition, and the concomitant quality gradients, was greatly inclined toward amorous-erotic pursuits. Vives declares: "Es el amor un sentimiento cálido y nace con facilidad en los temperamentos y disposiciones cálidas [youth], y los mismos en circunstancias de lugar, tiempo y acciones de ese mismo carácter." [5]

The natural heat of young men, then, was greatly raised when they fell in love; conversely, because of their heat, they were more apt to become enamored. And with love came joy, also a hot passion, but one 'chemically alloyed' with moisture. Thus natural and accidental sources, together with increased levels of moisture due to joy and hot blood (excessive heat made the blood 'boil' and swell its volume) brought about a rapid and drastic curtailment of reason. Joy, Huarte de San Juan tells us "...ha de humedecer el celebro y abajar el entendimiento," while blood, "...por ser húmeda ... echa a perder la facultad racional." [6] Lovers, hence, were hyperactive and foolish, blinded by their own humoral imbalance and, like Alonso, rendered incapable of seeing reality as it was.

When the natural body heat was raised by an onset of the amorous passions, the lover incurred a very grave hazard to his health in addition to the stultification of his reason. If the heat passed beyond tolerance levels it could burn or scorch the other humors, upset the spirits, and cause the unfortunate victim to contract a deadly metabolic condition known as unnatural melancholy. Huarte writes: "...el entendimiento ha menester que el celebro esté compuesto de partes subtiles y muy delicadas... y el mucho calor gasta y consume lo más delicado, y deja lo grueso y terrestre." (*Examen*, 144.) [7] The physician Andrés Velázquez tells

---

[5] Juan Luis Vives, *Tratado del alma*, ed. cit., II, 1255-a.

[6] Juan Huarte de San Juan, *Examen de ingenios para las ciencias*, ed. R. Sanz (Madrid, 1930), 140-141.

[7] Huarte de San Juan, *Examen*, 144. Cf. also Alfonso de Madrigal: "Quando es muy fuerte el amor, creçe el cuidado e el velar, é entonçe se quema

us that unnatural melancholy may be precipitated in three ways: "Esta enfermedad se haze en una de tres maneras, o siendo propria passion del celebro, de manera que en el se engendre este humor melancólico: por aver mucha intencion de calor interno, que asse y queme aquella sangre gruesa, negra, y melancholica: otras vezes se haze y viene a engendrar, por aver vicio comun."[8] Extreme heat, then, ignited all the humors and left them in a parched condition, seared and charred: thus there was created a black, heavy, cold and earthy mass which the doctors referred to as "atrabile." The process of combustion itself was, therefore, called "atrabilious adustion," and the new humor it produced, "atrabilious" or "melancholic adust." This noxious substance was unnatural melancholy as distinguished from natural melancholy, one of the four basic humors. It was held to be highly poisonous and represented one of the more lethal forms of sickness. The prognosis for recovery was very poor. The melancholic by adustion was easily identifiable by both physician and layman alike. Once the humors were reduced to cinders, deadly black vapors ascended to the shriveled brain producing a mental syndrome which could probably best be described in today's parlance as schizophrenia in that the victim lost all contact with reality. Yesteryear's medical texts abound in descriptions of men who believed themselves to be earthen pots, made of glass, or some other fragile substance, and would therefore break if they fell. At times they slipped into other personality roles and thought they were Caesar, Christ, and sundry other famous figures. In a word, their personalities were completely shattered, leaving them in a nebulous world of phantasy devoid of rational contact with their fellow men.

Two theories prevailed concerning the course of melancholic adustion. One affirmed that the patient passed through a manic

---

la sangre é se torna en malenconía, dañandose el pensamiento, é viene la torpedad, o mengua el seso, é sospecha lo que non puede ser." (*Tractado que fizo el muy excelente é eleuado Maestro en Santa Teología, Don Alfon, Obispo que fue de Avila que llamaban El Tostado... por el qual se prueba por la Santa Escriptura como al ome es necessario amar, é el que verdaderamente ama es necessario que se turbe*, in Bibliófilos Españoles, XXIX, 241. See also Jacques Ferrand, *Erotomania, or A Treatise Discoursing of the Essence, Causes, Symptomes, Prognostics, and Cure of Love or Erotique Melancholy*, tr. Edmund Chilmead (Oxford, 1640), 10.

[8] Andrés Velázquez, *Libro de la melancolía* (Sevilla, 1585), 57v.

stage characterized by unusual activity, levity, recklessness and a blind disregard for danger. In the early period the individual's behavior seems to be determined primarily by the prodigious heat that the combustion generates. At this point, reason has not yet been completely overthrown by distemperature. "When it is hot [unnatural melancholy] it maketh men merry madde..." says Elyot.[9] Timothy Bright affirms that if blood becomes inflamed, then the result is that the world of the unfortunate victim for a while becomes topsy-turvy, *el mundo al revés*, in which what is serious becomes playful: "If blood minister to this fire, every serious thing for a time, is turned into a iuest, and tragedies into comedies, and lamentations into gigges and daunces."[10] But when the volatile concoction cools, the patient sinks into a stupor, becomes withdrawn, and, in very severe cases, ultimately succumbs to death. The other opinion, held by such eminent physicians as Huarte, was that these stages alternated in cycles, the afflicted experiencing moments of relative, if euphoric, clarity which were followed by unusually intense feelings of sadness, isolation, etc. At least during this time he is capable of participating in human affairs, albeit with distorted vision.

It should be noted that the principal cause of the fearful adustion was heat: and nothing generated heat in such volume as love. If excessive temperature damaged the rational faculty (in conjunction with moisture), it also activated the imagination, causing it to "boil," says Huarte: "...el calor es el instrumento con que obra la imaginativa, porque esta calidad levanta las figuras y las hace bullir, por donde se descubre todo lo que hay que ver en ellas." (*Examen*, 121.) Thus lovers were foolish, but highly creative in their poetry to the beloved. Enormous heat not only enlivened the imagination, it also induced a somewhat unexplained power of prescience entirely unrelated to rational intelligence, Huarte tells us: "...por calentarse demasiado el celebro vienen muchos hombres a conocer lo que está por venir como son las sibilas." (*Examen*, 121.) Melancholics through adustion, like poets

---

[9] Thomas Elyot, *The Castel of Health*, Scholars Facsimiles and Reprints (New York, 1937), 73r.

[10] Timothy Bright, *A Treatise of Melancholy* (London, 1586), 111.

and lovers, shared in this transcendental knowledge of future events. Now a sure sign of grave illness was the occurrences of tortured and painful dreams. In his translation of the *Aphorisms* of Hippocrates, Alonso Manuel Sedeño de Mesa duly sets the Greek's affirmation into Spanish along with the cause of disturbed sleep: "Señales corporales de enfermedad: perder el color, sueño desigual, interrupto, sueños temerosos y desacostumbrados; porque semejantes sueños significan abundancia de humores gruesos, o que los espíritus están perturbados. [11]

Jerónimo Cortés is no less categorical in his description of melancholics: "...los tales acostumbran soñar cosas tristes y de pesar." (*Fisonomía*, 6.) Don Gaspar Navarro agrees emphatically with Cortés and his contemporaries: "...el melancólico sueña cosas negras, obscuras, tristes, y de muertos." [12] All of the learned doctors agreed, therefore, that a superabundance of heat overthrew the sovereignty of the rational faculty, incited the imagination to extraordinary activity, brought about at times a state of clairvoyance, and was the immediate source of adustion. They further held that the melancholy ensuing from the corruption of the humors was clearly recognizable by possession of knowledge not normally accessible to the healthy man, and by dark and terrifying nightmares.

Love sickness, was, then, no mere poetic figure but rather a legitimate malady. It should not be inferred that every lover necessarily was destined to fall into melancholy: but the atrabilious infection was a distinct possibility, and depending on the degree of infatuation, a decided probability. The fervent poetic mentality of the courtly posture, the agonizing suffering, the visions and insights of dreamlike nature, the rational blindness of Venus's flock, even the attractiveness of danger, are in part explainable by this background of 'scientific lore.' What is unique about the troubadours' legacy is that the love-possessed did not flee the onset of passion's syndrome in horror, but rather welcomed its appearance as a purifying heat that subtly burned away the natural impurities of the spirit leaving an essence of purest virtue, even though it was common knowledge that passion's flame could

---

[11] Alonso Manuel Sedeño de Mesa, *Traducción de los aphorismos de Hipocrates* (Madrid, 1699), 2v.

[12] Gaspar Navarro, *Tribunal de superstición ladina* (Huesca, 1631), 72r.

extinguish forever the enraptured soul and thus put out the light so brightly burning. But, then, love's delight was always accompanied by risks, and ecstasy would not be ecstasy without risk and courage.

The foregoing brief outline of the causes and partial symptomatology of love sickness has been set forth as the background within which the present study intends to examine the nature of Alonso's dream together with its dramatic impact. Because the audience knows that "de noche le mataron / al caballero" there occurs a major difference between the spectator's understanding and the hero's appraisal of his nightmare. Because of the superior knowledge two factors become important: first, the dream is obviously prophetic and, then, represents a moment of clairvoyance on the part of the protagonist, although he cannot recognize it as such, and, second, the dream is terrifying. The scene is divided into two parts. In the beginning the young man bemoans his suffering and agony caused by the necessary separation from Inés. Once again Lope affirms the courtly texture of Alonso's passion in the equations of living-dying, love-death, brought on by the absence that paradoxically draws the lover nearer to the beloved in spirit. Tello arrives and recounts his experiences during the masque. The aesthetic purpose of both recapitulations is to remind the spectator that Alonso's malady has increased and with it, of course, the heat which *amor* engenders. It is because of the secret love that events have taken their peculiar turn. Action and plot are thus tightly focused as cause and effect. Finally, the hero reveals his dream in a series of symbols that at once synthesize the entire dramatic complex and provide the final perspectives that commit the play to the inevitable movement toward tragedy.

The dreamer tells us of a hawk surprising a goldfinch which is pitifully torn to shreds in the larger bird's talons while the goldfinch's mate looks on helplessly. The symbolic equivalences are significant. The *jilguero* is a brightly colored bird whose very brilliance adds majesty to the world in which he lives: "...cuyas esmaltadas alas / con lo amarillo añadían / flores a las verdes ramas" (813-a.), in which beauty he is not unlike Alonso himself. It is important to realize that the protagonist is no ordinary lover, but rather enjoys a reputation of great esteem, indeed, like the goldfinch, a colorful individual who stands out in nature. The small bird is singing to its mate of love's sweet woe (813-a.), *because of which melody* the hawk, hidden in an almond tree, swoops down on its prey. We recall that this final scene of Act II begins with the hero's courtly lament intoning the *quejas de amor.* Since the hawk's natural weapons are so much more powerful than the defenses of its prey (813-b.), the flowers are speckled with the tiny songster's blood and his lovely plumage is scattered in the wind. (813-b.) The symbolic referends of the goldfinch, his song, and his mate are at once apparent. Likewise the fate of the *jilguero*, when measured against Alonso's traditional destiny, offers no difficulty. In this detail is seen the dream's prophecy.

The exact denomination of the hawk is more troublesome. It would be tempting to conclude that the goldfinch's more powerful executioner was Rodrigo whose function seems to correspond to that of the predator waiting in ambush. But this assumption would violate the temporal coordinate of drama in that the hero's death at the hands of his antagonist is an event yet to be witnessed. The refrain, for all of its prognostication, does not relate *how* the Knight will die, nor by whose hand. On the other hand, Rodrigo's one appearance in Act II distinctly casts him in the role of a villain intent on destroying whoever is the cause of Inés's coldness. Although the spectator at this point cannot know that Rodrigo will be the hawk, Lope has nevertheless shaped events and the anti-hero's character in such a way that the equation of the symbol with the rival is logically warrantable. The hawk symbol, however, certainly has another value related to the clarvoyant complexion of the dream itself. As we have seen, those who suffered hideous nightmares and suddenly acquired the power to envision the course of the future were believed to be afflicted with unnatural melancholy brought on by severe heat. Speaking of the various disturbances to which melancholics were singularly subject, Paré states: "...they are observed to see in the night Devils... dead corpses, and many other such things full of horror, by reason of a blacke vapour, diversely moving and disturbing the Braine." [13] And Du Laurens underscores the strange visionary ability of

---

[13] Ambroise Paré, *The Works of that famous Chirurgeon Ambrose Parey*, tr. Thomas Johnson (1634), quoted from J. B. Bamborough, *The Little World of Man* (London, 1952), 98.

melancholics: "...[they] oftentimes... foretell and forge very strange things in their imagination." [14] The dream is the second such experience that Alonso has related, the first having been the vision in the chapel. Thus by the end of Act II the symptoms of the dreaded melancholic adustion resulting from the excessive heat of passion become clearly visible in the foreshadowing which the dream expresses.

The terrible and accurate prophecy of Alonso's nightmare, then, in the seventeenth-century frame of reference, is explainable as a characteristic of love sickness. But illness, it must be remembered, can also be caused by witches. Especially during the late Middle Ages and the Renaissance there was a marked proclivity on the part of the masses to ascribe any kind of psychological or metabolic disorder to the evil knowledge of the devil's allies. Sprenger and Krämer report in the *Malleus* that in their experience untold numbers of people were strongly given to ascribing their maladies to the work of witchcraft:

> For countless men and women who were blind, or lame, or withered, or plagued with various infirmities, severally took their oath that they had strong suspicions that their illnesses, both in general and in particular, were caused by witches, and that they were bound to endure those ills either for a period or right up to their deaths. (*Malleus*, 139.)

Melancholy, natural and unnatural, was particularly suspected of being induced by diabolical infusion. So much so, in fact, that it became difficult during this time to distinguish medically and scientifically between a natural melancholy and possession by a devil or a spell cast by a witch. Meric Casaubon tells us: "How ordinary it is to mistake a natural melancholy for a Devil? And how much, too frequently, is both the disease increased, or made incurable; and the mistake confirmed, by many ignorant Ministers who take every motion, or phansie, for a suggestion of the De-

---

[14] André Du Laurens, *A Discourse of the Preservation of the Sight: of Melancolike Diseases: of Rheumes and of Old Age*, tr. Richard Surphlet (London, 1599), 100, in Shakespeare Association Facsimiles, No. 15 (Oxford, England, 1938).

vil?" [15] Unnatural melancholy, more specifically, was so destructive that it was often referred to as the *balneum diaboli,* which prompts Pedro Mercado to exclaim: "Si supiessedes el nombre que muchos antiguos le pusieron, escusaros y además: que la llamaron Demonio. Y tuvieron razón porque sus efectos son verdaderamente de demonio: amonestando siempre cosas que contradizen la salvación de el anima." [16] That unnatural melancholy smelled of brimstone and witches' potions was a logical corollary to the designs of the prince of darkness. The authors of the *Malleus* also describe how the devil can gain easy entrance into the organism through the distemperature of the humors, which paralyzes the rational faculty and thus renders the victim vulnerable to interior temptation. (*Malleus,* 50.) Navarro repeatedly points out that Lucifer is an expert physician, far more skilled than all the doctors together, and through the instrumentality of his minions is capable of inflicting the most acute physical infirmities: "Verdad es Catholica, que los Demonios son enemigos nuestros y pueden dañar, y hechizar, por los pactos que hazen con ellos los magos, hechizeras, y hechizeros, causando en los cuerpos enfermedades, y dolores; como lo enseña S. Agustín." (*Tribunal,* 62r.) The association between love, magic, and illness is boldly affirmed by the great and scholarly Robert Burton in the long section devoted to "Love Melancholy" in his *Anatomy of Melancholy:*

> In our time it is a common thing, saith Erastus, in his book *de Lamiis,* for witches to take upon them the making of philters, "to force men and women to love and hate whom they will, to cause tempests, diseases, &c. by charmes, spells, characters, knots." St. Hieronome proves that they can do it... Such instances I find in John Nider, *Formicar.* lib. 5. cap. 5. [17]

---

[15] Meric Casaubon, *A Treatise Proving Spirits, Witches, and Supernatural Operations by Pregnant Instances and Evidences* (London, 1672), in Christine Hole, *A Mirror of Witchcraft,* 31.

[16] Pedro Mercado, *Diálogos de philosophia natural y moral* (Granada, 1548), 150r.

[17] Robert Burton, *The Anatomy of Melancholy,* Everyman's Library (London, 1961), III, 130.

And elsewhere the English savant vigorously declares: "Heliodorus lib. 3 proves at large that love is witchcraft." (*Anatomy*, III, 85.)

There can be little doubt, then, that to the audiences for whom Lope wrote, Alonso's dream represented at once the progression of the hero's passion and the onset of unnatural melancholy as the inevitable consequence of his philocaption. Led, however, by Lope's portraiture of Fabia, the dramatist's skill in juxtaposing events, the brilliantly equivocal texture of the preceding masque, the analogical suggestion inherent in the scene with John and Alvaro, and conditioned by the corpus of current science and common knowledge, the *aficionados* of the Corrales would have understood forthwith that the dream was as symptomatic of the lover's malady as it was indicative of Fabia's hellish arts. The greater Alonso's passion and the more intense his secret love, the more he will stand in need of the *tercera*, and thus the higher the risk of psychological hemorrhage by adustion. And what better way to bring this about than to submerge the spirit of one so fair as Alonso in the dark and viscous liquid of the *balneum diaboli*? *Alcahuetería* was indeed the instrument of *brujería*. Therefore, the symbol of the hawk lying in wait for the call of love, when compared to the plot progression of the play from the beginning, refers, in the last analysis, to Fabia in whose design Rodrigo is but a tool.

In retrospect, Lope's organization of Act II presents an amazing symmetry. Two rather lengthy scenes (the *reja* and the 'charade') are followed by two short ones (Rodrigo-Fernando, Juan-Álvaro), and the Act is brought to a close with the hero's disclosure of his dream. In effect, there are three dramatic moments. The two short interruptions serve to verify the ironic composition of the more developed representations to which they are conceptually subordinated, although independent in time and place. Both the *reja* and charade sequences have in common an elaborate dialogue which requires the audience to differentiate appearance from reality, thus translating all that is seen and heard into an ironic interpretation. In short, the second jornada demands an act of *sobrentendimiento*. The tragic tension which unifies it is inherent in such a creative participation. From Tello's opening malaise onward we sense an atmosphere of impending disaster, because a love that becomes involved with hanged criminals, is under suspicion by a jealous rival, and born in a time of national concern about enemies from within, cannot survive for long in a society directed from above by an Álvaro de Luna and from below by a Fabia. Thus Alonso's prophetic and horrendous dream at the close of the Act substantiates the presentiment of a sinister mediation in the affairs of men. As we hear the sad tale of the helpless goldfinch, the turbulence that Lope has so carefully created throughout his play, for a moment breaks through to the surface, drawing the play and the drama into a single unity. It is here that the inner congruency of *cortesía, alcahuetería,* and *brujería* is most clearly defined, and that the tension of an ironic intuition yields finally to the certainty of a tragic anticipation.

ACT III

The morphology of Act III is divided into three principal dramatic moments. The first is constructed around the bullring and the activities presented there. The second section takes place after the celebration. It is composed of two parts: the love scene between Alonso and Inés, and the hero's return to his home and subsequent death. The final segment of action is a coda in which justice is meted out to Rodrigo and the preceding events are declared to be tragic, thereby justifying the play.

Scene one (i-ix)

We have seen that through the instrumentality of the protagonist's dream at the end of the second Act Lope begins to coalesce the two action masses. Essentially, this consists of a change from the coordination of fore and back perspectives to the unification of both in what appears to be at that point a cause and effect relationship. It is of utmost importance to understand the connection between events and time. Professor Soons's observation that "In Lope's plays the time of year is alway indicative and helps to reinforce the play's meaning in Christian terms..." is pertinent to our analysis. [1] The first objective indication that the hero's passion has begotten a Minotaur is revealed precisely on the eve of the festival honoring Christ's conversation with Nicodemus in which He alludes to His imminent Crucifixion which will liberate the new man. This is set forth in the third Chapter of John, vs. 12-17.

---

[1] C. A. Soons, *art. cit.*, 165.

That Lope arranged for our awareness of an inner turbulence in the hero to coincide with the time of the *fiesta* is clear in two ways. It is obvious that Alonso's nightmare was experienced prior to his description of it. Yet Lope withholds this information until the moment preceding the scenes which dramatize the bullfight. Secondly, the spectacle at the *corrida de toros* could just as plausibly have been held in honor of the King, with no reference to a religious festival. But it is the King who has decided to attend the activities in Medina during this time. Indeed, if we review for a brief moment the temporal coordinate of all previous actions, it is clear that the love affair itself was engendered only a short while prior to the beginning of the *cañas*. The first mention of the time of action occurs on the lips of Fernando in the second Act. Rodrigo has just confessed that a "mortal desmayo/ cubre mi amor de celos y de enojos." (808-b.) To comfort his companion, Fernando replies, "Salid galán para la Cruz de Mayo." (808-b.) The effect is to link the birth of Rodrigo's jealousy to a specific date in time. Likewise the masque during which Inés pretends to initiate her preparation for the new life takes place either on the same day as the bullfight or the day before, since the time is relatively unclear at this point. It should be further noted that the charade begins and ends with references to the annual spectacle. (809-a, and 810-b.) In short, then, everything that has been set before our eyes from the middle of Act II must be witnessed with the holy day, and all it represents, in mind. To understand the creative rationale for such a meticulous coordination one must examine the peculiar pattern of the *corrida* action, the symbolism inherent in the contest, the outcome of the hero's performance, and, most important, the morphological organization of this series of scenes.

The action begins *in medias res*. The stage is supposed to represent either an ante-room or the area outside of the bullring. Rodrigo and Fernando enter directly from the arena, and we learn at once that Lady Fortune has smiled as prodigiously on Alonso this day as she has frowned outrageously on the hero's antagonist. Rodrigo remarks, "Para el de Olmedo, en efeto,/ guardó suertes la fortuna." (814-a.) Alonso can do no wrong (814-a.), which leads Fernando to declare, "Un hombre favorecido,/ Rodrigo, todo lo acierta." (814-a.) From the wings of the stage the thunderous ovation that the crowd is rendering to the protagonist's incredible exploits is heard.[2] Fernando advises his companion that they must return to the fray since the spectators will be expecting their reappearance. Rodrigo comments sadly that there is no hope of his executing any *paso* with even the slightest *maestría:* indeed, to his mind, a return to the ring might well mean death, or at least a bad goring which, to be sure, would make him the town laughing stock. (814-b.) Despite this premonition of imminent danger Rodrigo does, nevertheless, return to the contest. The scene changes abruptly after a short dialogue between Alonso and his servant. Tello leaves the stage to deliver his master's message to Fabia. We learn then that unlike all the other townspeople, she has not cared to participate in the day's amusements, remaining behind, and as it were, in the background. It is here that Lope proves that his conception of Fabia is fundamentally quite different from Rojas's Celestina. As the lackey proceeds along the way discoursing with himself, he reminds us of Pármeno and Sempronio intent on robbing Calisto's physician of the chain which their master had given to her, for just such a thought has crossed Tello's mind also. But he dismisses it forthwith, realizing that Fabia, wiser even than Circe, Medea, and Hecate combined (815-b.), would doubtless have divined his criminal intentions if Lucifer had not already told her in advance. He arrives, speaks with *la madre,* and departs.

Once again we are returned to the *plaza de toros* to witness the utter downfall and disgrace of Rodrigo. He has fallen from his mount, only to be rescued by his arch-rival. His wretched showing in the presence of the Medina citizenry is painful enough, but to have suffered such ignominious defeat before Inés and the King is more than the unfavored suitor can bear, especially since Alonso dispatched with little or no effort the very bull that unseated him. The profoundly chagrined antagonist, embarrassed

---

[2] The physical disposition of the stage is correlative to the effect Lope wishes to achieve. With the crowd in the background, their shouts and cheers literally flood the stage with sound, surrounding the unfortunate Rodrigo with the news of Alonso's success. The two men are, so to speak, lost and virtually forgotten in the wave of good luck which the hero enjoys. Thus, their isolation contrasts vividly with the fervor and excitement within. Elsewhere Lope has made use of the physical plan of his stage in much the same manner. See my article: "*Fuenteovejuna*: Its Platonic Conception and Execution," *Studies in Philology*, LVIII, 179-192.

and dejected by the capricious turn of events, catalogues the factors that have conspired to ruin his candidacy: "¡Qué de afrentas, qué de penas, / qué de agravios, qué de enojos, / qué de injurias, qué de celos, / qué de agüeros, qué de asombros!" (816-b.) His anguished appraisal of such a miserable predicament, stated here as a list of grievances directed against nature itself, is an effective reminder of the strange interplay of human emotion and the powerful forces surrounding the action of the play that appear to have motivated the unusual course of events. His final reaction to Alonso's good fortune, together with his own humiliation, resolves the suspended tension created in Act II when he confessed a *mortal desmayo*: now only the protagonist's death can soothe the sting of disgrace. After his fall there can be no uncertainty as to Alonso's fate nor to Rodrigo's role in that destiny. The first moment of Act III ends with a brief scene in which the King and his Constable discuss the *corrida,* thus providing a commentary on the action as seen by two relatively dispassionate witnesses.

Why has Lope so meticulously coordinated plot and time? Why does he interrupt the action in the arena with the brief scene with Tello and Fabia? How can we explain Fabia's absence from the festivities when all of Medina is present? Can we assume that Alonso is as superior to Rodrigo in the art of *tauromaquia* as the outcome of the *cañas* would appear to indicate? Indeed, is the anti-hero so much inferior to the hero in every measure?[3] However expert Alonso may be as a *torero,* we cannot suppose that Rodrigo is a novice at the art. There is an air of unreality about the outcome of the bullfight which tacitly suggests that Alonso's performance *on this day* exceeds the measure of his skill, albeit his uncommon success is worthy of "seven hundred hurrahs"

---

[3] Pedro's acceptance of Rodrigo as a prospective husband in the first Act would appear to suggest that the 'native son' is certainly acceptable socially to a father who admittedly wants the best possible marriage for his daughter. It would be difficult to affirm that Rodrigo's passion for Inés is any less genuine than that of Alonso. And, to be sure, his conduct is more honorable than that of his rival with respect to the proper forms of courtship. All of which is to say that Lope has not entirely portrayed the antagonist as a classical villain up to this point. There is, on the contrary, a hint of sympathy for the unfortunate suitor who pays homage to his *midons* in Act I despite his awareness that the lady has rejected him. (800-a.)

(814-b.), and the superlative judgment heard from the wings that "Nadie en el mundo le iguala." (814-b.) The hero's exaggerated good fortune prompts don Alvaro de Luna to say in admiration: "No sé en él cuál es mayor, / la aventura o el valor, / aunque es el valor notable." (817-b.) The constable's remark, the observation of an objective by-stander, casts a sheen of astonished disbelief over an accomplished fact. Enough has been said to point out that the superiority of Alonso over Rodrigo is, in every aspect in which the two men are comparable, more apparent than real. That the Olmedino is somewhat more attractive, somewhat the better *caballero*, cannot be denied, although it is a question of a narrow range of degree rather than the opposition of wholly unmatched antagonists. If the outsider has bested the insider in the arena, his success in gaining Inés's affection is no less complete. The love competition is reflected in the *corrida,* and in the parallel which Fernando and Rodrigo draw between the two contests is mirrored the very logic of courtly tragedy:

Rodrigo:	Abrióle el amor la puerta,
	y a mí, Fernando, el olvido.
	Fuera desto, un forastero
	luego se lleva los ojos.
Fernando:	Vos tenéis justos enojos.
	El es galán caballero,
	mas no para escurecer
	los hombres que hay en Medina.
Rodrigo:	La patria me desatina;
	mucho parece mujer
	en que lo proprio desprecia,
	y de lo ajeno se agrada. (814-a.)

Thus, as Rodrigo states, the favor Alonso enjoys with the crowd, like Inés's attraction to him, both geographically and morally, is related to his position as a *forastero.*

The analogical identity of ring and *reja* is verbally fixed in the dialogue between Fernando and Rodrigo, and the key to the coordination of plot and time must be sought in this fusion of both actions in terms of a bullfight with its concomitant victor and vanquished. Alonso is now at the zenith of his development, for he has won the lady, the accolades of Medina, and the king himself. Yet because of these triumphs he has also unwittingly appointed his own executioner. Inés is the figure common to both contests, and it is thus her presence in each, literally and figuratively, that sets the ultimate course of the tragedy. As Rodrigo lies prostrate on the sand, he looks up to see if there is not some small semblance of pity on her face. What he sees in her countenance reminds him of Nero's glee at the holocaust of Rome (816-b.), although but a moment later the lady's face betrays unblushing love and admiration for Alonso. It is because of the humiliation in the ring, therefore, that the antagonist discovers his second defeat: the loss of Inés. The conjunction of disgrace with the realization that her love is reserved for another transforms Rodrigo from a simple anti-hero into the instrument of death. Had Inés not attended the *corrida,* he would not have learned with certainty that the outsider was twice a rival, and — perhaps — might not have been so impelled toward murder.[4]

The relationship of these two analogical actions to the time of year is defined by Fabia's role in each. The Reverend Montague Summers writes that during the trials held at Logroño in 1610 several Navarrese witches confessed that the dates of sabbats were usually fixed to correspond to the principal religious feasts of the year, namely, Easter, Epiphany, Ascension Day, Corpus Christi, the Purification and Nativity of Our Lady, the Assumption, All Saints Day, and the major festival of Saint John the Baptist. (Summers, *History,* 113.) A triumph for Satan at any time set aside for piety, it was believed, was particularly gratifying to the prince of darkness because it was all the more offensive to the Creator. The *Malleus* is most specific on this point:

> ...they [witches] are wont to practice their witchcraft at the more sacred times of the year, especially at the Advent of Our Lord, and at Christmas. First, that by

---

[4] It should be carefully noted that during the one appearance of Rodrigo in Act II, he states in effect that he has grave *suspicions* that Alonso is the source of Inés's disdain. (808-a.) The note of incertitude is further reinforced when Fernando remarks: "Son celos, don Rodrigo, una quimera / que se forma de envidia, viento y sombra, / con que lo incierto imaginado altera..." (808-b.) Finally, the impersonal *quien* emphasizes the status of suspicion in Rodrigo's mind when he says: "Yo he de matar a quien vivir me cuesta..." (808-b.) Thus, Inés's face is the mirror in which the truth of his apprehensions is reflected.

such means they may make men guilty of not only perfidy, but also sacrilege, by contaminating whatever is divine in them; and that so they may the more deeply offend God their Creator, damn their own souls, and cause many more to rush into sin. (*Malleus*, 116.)

Lope has carefully synchronized the genesis of this love affair, the onset of Alonso's sickness, the brilliant performance of "La gala de Medina" in the *plaza*, and Rodrigo's humiliation and resultant commitment to Alonso's murder with the festivities of the Cruz de Mayo. Thus the conditions and events that will lead to the hero's eventual death materialize efficiently in the midst of a religious celebration which is the most propitious time for a witch to concert all her diabolical knowledge for the downfall of a Christian Knight. Here is the reason for the structural equivalence of the bullfight and the love duet. As previously mentioned, it is due to the outcome of the *cañas*, that Rodrigo learns of his antagonist. And Lope has carefully articulated the action at the ring in such a way that Fabia's hand in what happens there is powerfully suggested. First, we recall, Inés is the means of Rodrigo's discovery. At the end of the charade in Act II, it was Fabia who gave her permission for Inés to attend the spectacle: "...doy licencia, por lo menos / para estas fiestas, por ser / *jugatoribus paternos*." (810-b.) More specifically, however, the interplay between scene organization and event is a replica of the first unsuccessful rendezvous of the lovers in Act I. There, the fatal confusion occasioned by the ribbon took place at the same time the *tercera-bruja* was busily engaged in procuring the hanged man's tooth. Likewise, at the most crucial instant of the bullring action, when Rodrigo finally decides to face the charging beast one more time, Lope abruptly changes scene to Fabia's quarters. What happens in Tello's visit is the simple delivery of his master's message — *which could have been effected without a change of scene.* The fleeting thought about robbery in the servant's mind is quickly cancelled on remembering that Fabia is invulnerable by virtue of her vast knowledge. Thus Lope introduces this extended *aparte* with a reference to Fabia's witchcraft. The aesthetic purpose of the scene is to interpose once again the witch's image. Fabia, we must remember, is always seen either in the background or in a series of disguises and poses. Lope returns the audience immediately to the suspended action in the arena, where the first words we hear are "Cayó don Rodrigo." (816-b.) The anti-hero's fall, therefore is juxtaposed with the brief insert that moves Fabia into center stage. This concatenation of events reinforces the implied suggestion that in her mysterious manner the *medianera* has marshalled the forces of nature and twisted human disposition in such a way as to make Alonso's glory and Rodrigo's maximum misfortune coincide in time and space. Indeed, the antagonist's disaster answers the witch's seemingly playful question to Tello: "¿Qué yo tus hazañas causo? / Basta, que no lo sabía." (816-a.) The full impact of its oblique irony is experienced when the dramatist resumes the action in the bullring.

With the close of Scene one, Lope has achieved an integration of the components of tragedy in that the mechanics of catastrophe are set forth. The energy generated by the admixture of inevitability and incertitude gives way to the tension of imminence as Rodrigo's role in the tragic complexion is stated categorically. At this moment he becomes the executor of Fabia's design, and in so portraying him Lope fuses the recessed drama of occult activity with the play of courtly love. The full orchestration of events, characters, and time is now complete. It is due precisely to the hero's passion and secret courtship that Rodrigo now resolves to murder his tormentor. The classic pattern of the powers of *brujería* becomes concordant with the courtly doctrine of love and danger, passion and death. The complicated and intricate chain of apparent coincidence that began with Rodrigo's presence at the *reja*, and proceeded through his gaining possession of the ribbon, the loss of his cape which was the cause of suspicion, Inés's spur-of-the-moment resolve to "take the veil," Alonso's dream, his incredible day in the ring, Rodrigo's miserable performance at the same event, and the heroine's presence among the spectators, thus fall, at this point, into a clearly discernible design of internal adjustment leading unerringly to the antagonist's obsession. The anticipation of the Savior's crucifixion which the *fiesta* celebrates likewise heralds the coming demise of the hero. What more convenient time than this for a witch to unleash the pent-up fury of her apostasy in order to demonstrate her master's power despite Jesus's sacred mission? The confluence of drama and play through which Lope has accommodated a conjunction of the occult with the illicit, brilliantly illuminates the emerging shape of high tragedy.

Scene two (x-xxiii)

The second dramatic moment of the last Act initiates the final phase of the tragic syntax. The ciphers of catastrophe stand out clearly from the end of Act II. Scene two falls naturally into two parts: the last rendezvous and leavetaking, and the murder of the young knight. It is in this scene that Lope will realize the *peripetia* and *anagnorisis*. We recall that remarkably little dialogue has passed between the hero and his lady on the subject of marriage. Indeed, from virtually the beginning of the drama the question of matrimony has been hushed. In Act I, Rodrigo presented himself to don Pedro as a desirable candidate for the hand of Inés, which brought about the charade which is still in effect. The reason for this peculiar state of affairs is clear from the courtly directive of the love duet. Implicit in the mystique of *eros* is a well camouflaged understanding that the dance of love should not end, that its ecstatic enjoyment be of infinite duration, in short, eternally gratifying. Passion has a distinct beginning, and a sublime purpose, but no resolution. Or so goes the theory and proposed practice of love.

Yet the annals of the *gay saber* are full of palinodes in which the once ardent lover has either renounced the blessed suffering for a more solitary tranquillity, or else frankly returned to the social matrix by marrying the once distant lady. There were many reasons for the betrayal of Amor, not the least of which was probably an eventual *ennui* which such a monotonous game could create. More important, however, the avowed end of courtly doctrine carried within itself seeds of an entirely unforeseen spiritual flowering. If the objective of intense passion was to produce a condition of purity and transcendent beauty of spirit, then it followed that in due course the pull of the flesh would be dissolved in the new condition of radiant sublimation. As courtly love supposed a metamorphosis from *lascivia* to *eros,* the distinction between pure passion and pure love likewise became blurred. Thus it was possible for Cupid's flame, having burned away the impurities of the flesh, to undergo a transformation leading back to Christian marriage. Such a love would represent neither illicit passion, however pure, nor conventional matrimony, but rather a rarified connubial life brought forth from passion and adjusted to Christian *caritas* centered on a mutual sharing of the passionate experience within a Christian frame of reference. In other words, if courtly passion could engender a catharsis of the soul and hence a new spirituality, then marriage need no longer be envisioned as a mere formality instituted to control and sanctify primitive biology. From pure love and its theoretical effects, therefore, true love expressed as a union of souls, could be attained. In short, courtly love was supposed to bring about a change in the psychology of its votaries, and in that change the beginnings of romantic love within marriage lay inherent. Whether the medieval troubadours might have applauded such a development of their erotic gnosticism is debatable, but their latter-day heirs in the sixteenth and seventeenth centuries certainly did not see a necessary contradiction in the joining of pure passion — *amor purus* — and Christian union. That such a refined status might have been the exception does not injure the hypothesis of its possibility.[5] Perhaps no dramatist of the period was more aware that passion might lead to true love and marriage than Lope himself. This peculiar dialectic of love was an integral part of his literary inheritance and, to be sure, a truth drawn from experience. In *El poder vencido y amor premiado* we read: "Y no hay verdadero amor, / si no es el del casamiento, / porque tiene fundamento / en lo eterno del honor." (NRAE, VIII, 559-a.) True love, he says in *El peregrino en su patria* "solo mira al fin honesto: porque el que le tiene en el deleite es común con los animales." (Madrid, 1733, 239.) More specifically the compatibility of passion and marriage

---

[5] The Golden Age theater provides abundant evidence that passion and marriage could be compatible concepts. Blanca and García of *Del rey abajo ninguno* appear to be just such a couple, harmoniously married with passion yet burning brightly. At the end of Act I, García invites his beloved into the "garden" of love and mutual solace. And Blanca brings the Act to a close with the same metaphor. In Alarcón's *La verdad sospecha*, Jacinta longs to know the soul of the man to whom she has been contracted in marriage, reflecting the desirability in her mind of a more personal experience with the betrothed prior to marriage. (See p. 545 of the text in Alpern and Martel, *Diez Comedias*.)

is clearly set forth in Scene two. It is here that the delightful and illicit *danza de amor* begins to evolve into the more sophisticated expression described above. Unlike that of Calisto, Alonso's love has not descended into the flesh but has, rather, remained chaste and developed into a consciousness that marriage would put an end to his suffering yet not compromise the new spiritual relationship.

The time of day is sunset, the twilight hours following the afternoon's festivities, or so we gather from Alonso's remark: "Y lo dice el resplandor / que da el sol a las estrellas." (817-b.) This final meeting of Inés and her beloved, then, unlike the other trysts, begins while there are still a few lingering rays of sun in the heavens, and ends with the onset of night — a significant change in background. As usual, Tello accompanies his master. The servant's exit from the stage is also symbolic. He does not simply leave by way of the wings, but rather through a door into the house. Tello's physical act of entry graphically represents by way of contrast, the fact that Alonso does not enjoy this liberty; he is, literally, shut out from the abode of his *midons*. The door and Tello's passage through it function as correlatives to Alonso's state of mind at this point. Comparing his servant's freedom with his own immobility he remarks: "¿Cuándo, Leonor, podré entrar / con tal libertad aquí?" (818-a.) From her response we learn that the matter of marriage may well be close at hand. Alonso's brilliant performance in the ring, she tells him (818-a.), has earned the admiration of don Pedro, although a few lines farther on, Inés informs the audience that her father has the hero in mind for Leonor. (818-a.) Yet both maidens know that if Alonso and Inés will only declare their love for one another to the old man, in the words of Leonor, "en sabiendo vuestro amor, / sabrá escoger lo mejor, / como estimarlo después," (818-a.) since his heart is already inclined toward the young *galán*. (818-a.) Pedro's interest in Alonso as a husband for Leonor is due, of course, to the fact that he is still under the impression that Inés will shortly take her vows. Lope thus emphasizes the game-like nature of the affair in so far as Inés, Alonso, and Leonor as well, are aware that there is no real obstacle to marriage other than a self-imposed one. It is dramatically significant that the playwright remind his audience of this relationship now, for Alonso is soon to die precisely because of the passion that has been engendered by the *danza de amor*, which has no rationale in the facts of existence. With the very mention of the possibility of matrimony, then, we begin to sense that the moment of climax is at hand, because we know that this love is fated to be eternal, and marriage, therefore, would deprive it of this vital dimension. It is at this juncture — when the 'threat' of union materializes — that the spectator can best see Lope's accommodation of the logic of courtly love to plot disposition.

With Inés's arrival at the *reja* we move into the final phase of the tragic tale. The hero and his lady linger for a while in the now feeble light of day. Alonso informs her that he must depart forthwith to tell his parents of his well-being after the fight, lest they believe he has been injured. He takes his leave, is confronted by a specter, and finally is ambushed by Rodrigo, mortally wounded, and dies still on the road to his home in Olmedo. These three events — the leavetaking, the confrontation with the ghost, and the murder — concretize the final ironic and symbolic vision toward which all preceding actions have been oriented. From the time of Inés's arrival at the window and of the hero's last words, Lope achieves the emergence of Alonso as a truly tragic figure and thus defines the relationships between love and death.

Like the previous meetings, this one takes place at night, or rather twilight, in such a way that the departure of the hero coincides with the coming of the darkness. Lope again avails himself of the characteristic rhetoric of *la cortesía* that we have examined in previous scenes. In the lengthy gloss of the "Coplas antiguas" (818-b-819-a.) the young lover expresses his pain as a suspension between life and death: "Así parto muerto y vivo, / que vida y muerte recibo." (818-b) In the course of the conversation it becomes apparent that the protagonist has reverted to the same state of mind which he described in the dream narration at the end of Act II. We learn that his imagination has been troubling him of late, that he has been afflicted with a deep sadness that seems to announce the proximity of death; and, in addition, a peculiar form of fear stemming from the envy of his *contrarios*, he affirms, has made its presence felt. Here is the magnificent Alonso, only moments ago acclaimed for his incredible valor in the ring, now describing a condition of profoundest melancholia and fear. The feature distinguishing this state of clairvoyance from the earlier ones is that the victim *recognizes consciously* his premonitions are true, that death is now very near indeed. Nowhere perhaps does the ironic ambivalence inherent in courtly figures stand out in such relief. As the young man speaks, there appears to be another voice revealing itself through his very body, creating the impression that the speaker is writing his own fate in the book of life: "Ya para siempre me privo, / de verte, y de suerte vivo, / que mi muerte presumiendo, / parece que estoy diciendo: / 'Señora, aquesta te escribo'." (818-b.)

Such a transcendent vision into the course of the future clearly signals the final stages of the terrible love sickness. Lope's audiences would surely have recognized in Alonso's words, first the certitude that he had reached an advanced stage of unnatural melancholy and was indeed gravely ill, and that his clairvoyance was remarkably accurate in its prognostication of his imminent demise. All the medical authorities of the period agreed that prevision was an undeniable symptom of the disorder. Robert Burton alludes to the principal signs of the syndrome as Lope has dramatized it:

> Or as Lod. Mercatus proves, by reason of inward vapours, and humours from blood, choler, etc..., diversely mixed, they apprehend and see outwardly as they suppose, divers images, which indeed are not. As they that drink wine think all runs round, when it is in their own brain; so it is with these men, the fault and cause is inward, as Galen affirms, madmen and such as are near death, *quas extra se videre putant imagines, intra oculos habent...* Or else... the organs, corrupt by a corrupt phantasy, as Lemnius, lib. 1, cap. 16 well quotes, "cause a great agitation of spirits and humours, which wander to and from in all the creeks of the brain, and cause such apparitions before their eyes. *One thinks he reads something written in the moon,* as Pythagoras is said to have done of old; another smells brimstone, hears Cerberus bark;... (*Anatomy*, I, 425-426, italics mine.)

Sadness, especially sadness with no objective cause, fear, and sudden seizures of unnatural insight were the symptoms of acute melancholic poisoning, the natural metabolic disturbance of one whose constitution had become overheated by the erotic passions.

Alonso, as he appears now, in this last farewell to his beloved, displays all three to a marked degree. It is precisely the pervading sadness emanating from the young hero which infuses an atmosphere of tragically tense expectancy into this scene.[6]

The relationship of medical cause and effect should be set forth here in order to avoid the fallacy of imposing a modern psychological interpretation on Alonso's distinctly Renaissance infirmity. It might be easily argued that the protagonist's subliminal fear of Rodrigo is the true seat of his anxiety and that his great sadness is the outer indication of this submerged concern for his antagonist, especially since he states "la envidia de mis contrarios" (818-b.) has become a source of some preoccupation. In this view Rodrigo would represent the origin, and the sadness and fear the effects. That the anti-hero cannot be considered a causative factor of Alonso's uneasiness is clearly explained in the following segment of action when the Knight dismisses his rival on the grounds that Rodrigo owes his very life to Alonso, and, being of *buena sangre,* could not possibly harbor malice toward one who has snatched him from the arms of death in the bullring. (819-b.) It is unlikely, moreover, that Alonso should fear the very man whom he has bested in the ring. In every regard the hero has proved himself superior to his adversary and has no cause to tremble before either man or beast. This has been more than demonstrated during the events of the afternoon. When the shade makes its appearance, the young man remarks: "¡Que un hombre me atemorice / no habiendo temido a tantos!" (819-b.)

In Alonso's mind there is no objective reason to fear Rodrigo, and this is precisely the point Lope wishes to stress. Rather it is

---

[6] Elsewhere in his immense production Lope has left a wealth of information that demonstrates his knowledge of the medical lore of his period. Cf., for example, the following extracts with Alonso's leavetaking: "La fiera melancolía / es estar triste sin causa..." (*La quinta de Florencia,* RAE, XV, 363.) "Quien está triste, / ¿cómo puede decir que salud tiene? / Que entre los nombres que escribieron médicos / en las escuelas de la antigua Atenas, / de las enfermedades de los hombres, / la tristeza está cerca del primero. / Las pasiones del ánimo merecen / nombres de enfermedad, pues comunican / al cuerpo sus dolores y cuidados, / alterando el gobierno con que viven / y causando notables accidentes." (*La prueba de los ingenios,* RAE, XIV, 189.) Casilda of *Peribáñez* tells the Comendador that she thinks he is near death because he sees visions. (Ed. F. C. Sainz de Robles, I, 757-a.)

because of the eery sadness and fear that Alonso dimly suspects his adversary's unfathomable envy, and subsequently discards this hypothesis as illogical. Thus, at the end of the nocturnal farewell, he remarks to Inés that his premonitions are "sueños y fantasías, / si bien falsas ilusiones." (819-a.) His own explanation corresponds perfectly to the day's conception of the psychology of melancholy. Vives affirms: "Vemos tristes a personas melancólicas aunque nada les ocurra y sin que sepan darse cuenta del motivo." (*Tratado, op. cit.*, II, 1303-a) Robert Burton would have recognized immediately the cause of Alonso's misgivings and sadness: "The symptoms of the mind are superfluous and continual cogitations; for when the head is heated, it scorcheth the blood, and from thence proceed melancholy fumes, which trouble the mind." (*Anatomy*, I, 410.) Pedro Mercado states that excessive heat results in adustion which causes the victim to fall into paralyzing sadness and crippling fear, and these two effects, in turn, aggravate the melancholic poisoning itself, thus setting up a kind of circular chemistry which "...es causa de las ymaginaciones que padecen."[7] The fumes of adustion, then, attack both the reason and the imagination, deadening the one, exciting the other, and suspending the entire spiritual metabolism between *tristitia* and *metus*. Thus the fact that Alonso mentions his apprehensions about Rodrigo at this point must be understood as a projection onto the antagonist of the general seizure of fear that accompanies distemperature. Rodrigo becomes, so to speak, a focal point of anxiety, a symptom of mental illness rather than a cause. Alonso's uneasiness concerning Rodrigo proves, of course, to be accurate, but it is characteristic of the tragic hero that he cannot recognize truth when he sees it.

If there were any lingering doubts about the hero's malady, what now occurs on stage categorically affirms the extent of the disorder. The image of Alonso which Lope has created during the last conversation with Inés represents the dramatist's understanding of an essentially schizophrenic condition in that the young man's conscious mind rationally verbalizes the supra- or sub-conscious vision of his own death. This psychological split

---

[7] Pedro Mercado, *Diálogos de philosophia* (Granada, 1558), 155v.

is stated as a rational presentation of an irrational experience — that is, clairvoyance — and expressed poetically as if the protagonist's conscious mind were reading or writing an extraterrestrial communication. Burton describes this phenomenon as an inner voice: "...he [the patient] thinks something speaks or talks within him, or to him,..." (*Anatomy*, I, 387.) The *reja* scene prepares the way for the appearance of the ghost and the *labrador* which follow it in so far as the last rendezvous reveals the presence of unnatural inner turmoil in the hero's mind. When Inés's lover takes his farewell this ferment surges forth into dramatic objectification as a shade, and later as a most mysterious chthonic voice, the peasant. Whereas in the previous scene Alonso said that it *seemed* he was writing his discourse with Inés, here the ultimate sign of melancholic distemper is manifested in the dark apparition which confronts the young man. The irrational now assumes material form and confirms the validity of the clairvoyant trance which preceded it.

According to the psychological theory of the period, prolonged atrabilious congestion would eventually produce a total rupture of the psyche and constitution of the victim. Burton observes: "They are afraid of some loss, danger, that they shall surely lose their lives, ...and all they have, but why they know not." (*Anatomy*, I, 386.) "...he suspects everything he hears or sees to be a devil, or enchantment, and imagineth a thousand chimeras and visions, which to his thinking he certainly sees, bugbears, talks with black men, ghosts, goblins, etc." (*Anatomy*, I, 387.) Du Laurens records his experience with an ardent lover who paid continual court to his own shade. (*Discourse*, 120-122.) Pedro Mercado also writes of one who was convinced he was already dead: "Yo soy testigo de lo que agora diré. Que via uno hazer por si mismo tan gran llanto, que diez hombres no lo podíamos apaziguar: y preguntándole porque lloraua respondió, que lo avían muerto los criados de un vicario." (*Diálogos*, 151 v.) Nor was Lope himself any less aware than the physicians of the nature of this contagion. Rodrigo, speaking of his daughter Florinda, remarks: "Seis años la tuve enferma / melancólica y turbada, / Porque decía que vía / muertos, moros, y fantasmas,." (*Rodrigo, el último godo*, RAE, VII, 90.) In *Guardar y guardarse,* don Félix tells the King about the peculiar behavior of the Admiral of Aragón: "Melancólico al fin, traidor me nombra, / Huye y se espanta de su misma sombra." (BAE, XLI, 190.)

The brief appearance of the ghost, for all its effectiveness, is reinforced a short time later when a voice is heard from the wings of the stage, *desde lejos,* singing a ballad about the murder of the hero, and of the shade which announced the coming fall. Like the ghost, this figure is mysterious: he comes out of the night, apparently from nowhere, delivers his message and seems to vanish again into the blackness that pervades the scene. The air of unreality is set forth clearly by the now terrified hero when he remarks that this voice appears not to be that of any ordinary peasant: "...y no es rústico el acento." (820-b.) To add to the aura of the supernatural, Alonso is startled by the peasant's instrument on which he strums his sad song. (820-b.) Both the *labrador* and the shade arrive on a stage bathed in darkness and shadow. This use of semi-obscurity places emphasis on the auditory rather than the visual experience. Alonso exclaims: "¡Qué escuridad! Todo es / horror..." (820-b.) Since the ghost and the rustic are present on the stage only for short intervals, Lope obviously intended for them to be seen briefly, in such a way that their discourse gives the impression of originating in the darkness which surrounds the young Knight and objectifies the atrabilious adustion that has so disturbed his mind. Lope has consistently alternated light and shadow to reinforce the technical accommodation of tragedy's underlying metaphysical irony, for the ritual of tragedy celebrates the confrontation of the rational with the irrational, of the expected with the unexpected. If man has one weapon to counterbalance his inherent fragility, it is his intelligence. But intelligence, too, is physically corruptible and subject to disease, error, and wrong judgement. This is at least partially why the dramatist has included the shade and the strange peasant at this vital point just prior to the death of the hero: to the spectator of the playhouses, their presence can only indicate the utter helplessness of Alonso as he stands now on the threshold of eternity.

Lope could well have disposed of Alonso without the inclusion of the phantoms. The night is intensely dark and Rodrigo lies in ambush with his henchmen. Moreover, the young Knight travels alone to his home, and would be no match for his pursuers. The rationale for such a disposition of events and scenes lies in the ironic dualism of tragedy that exalts the protagonist despite — indeed, because of — his *hamartia*. It must be admitted that in the last analysis, Alonso's present pathetic condition can be traced back to his surrender to passion. If this love has gone underground it is due to Fabia's entrepreneurship. To feel the full impact of her presence at this time we must return to the Renaissance conceptions of disease and the goetic sciences, since Lope has skillfully joined these two fields of association in the complex circumstances which attend the last moments on earth of Alonso.

To begin with, the witch was a notorious coordinator of all the occult and destructive forces in nature that lie hidden just beneath the surface of order and form. Like the demon, Quiñones Benavente writes, she understands the secret nature of all things and can draw forth from objects a new autonomy not vouchsafed to ordinary human beings:

> ...en los guisados de los manjares, en la confección de las medicinas y farmacos: assí el demonio, que es de mejor artificio y solercia, y que no ay confección que no sepa, alcance y conozca... de tal manera puede componer y disponer, y mexclar las causas naturales, que produzcan más admirables efetos que ellas mismas por si pudieran produzir... [8]

Armed with such sinister knowledge derived from the devil, the malefactors took a particular interest in the melancholic humors, natural, and especially unnatural. Burton explains the reason for their consuming preoccupation:

> He [the devil] begins first with the phantasy and moves that so strongly that no reason is able to resist. Now phantasy he moves by mediation of humours although many physicians are of opinion that the devil can alter

---

[8] Juan de Quiñones Benavente, *Tratado de las langostas* (Madrid, 1619), 42v. Burton's description of the powers of evil angels coincides with his appraisal of the witch, both of whom derive their dominion from the demon: "...they have understanding far beyond men, can probably conjecture and foretell many things: they can cause and cure most diseases, deceive our senses;... They can produce miraculous alterations in the air, and most wonderful effects, conquer armies, help, further, hurt, cross, and alter human attempts and projects (*Dei permissu*) as they see good themselves." (*Anatomy*, I, 186.)

the mind, and produce this disease of himself. *Quibusdam medicorum visum,* saith Avicenna, *quod melancholia contigat a daemonio.* Of the same mind is Psellus and Rhasis the Arab... "that this disease proceeds especially from the devil, and from him alone." Arculanus... Rhasis... Aelianus Montaltus... Daniel Sennertus confirm as much. ...the devil, spying his opportunity of such humors, drives them many times to despair, fury, rage, etc., mingling himself amongst them. This is that which Tertullian avers,... and which Lemnius goes about to prove. Agrippa and Lavater are persuaded that this humour invites the devil to it, wheresoever it is in extremity, and, of all other, melancholy persons are most subject to diabolical temptations and illusions, and most apt to entertain them, and the devil best able to work upon them. (*Anatomy,* I, 199-200.)

The problem of ghosts and apparitions was a vexing one at this time. To explain the supernatural, three principal theorems were in vogue. The question is of importance here because later on, Alonso, in the throes of death, remarks that he has paid little heed to the "avisos del cielo." (822-a.) It would be easy to conclude from this utterance that Lope meant for the *sombra* and the *labrador* to be understood as messengers of God. That their appearance may be envisioned as an expression of God's inscrutable design cannot be theologically denied, for all occurrences in the universe reveal the Providential Intelligence in one way or another. We shall return to this idea at another time. In the baroque view, however, it is unlikely that these events represented the direct intervention of the Maker in this affair. The second and third hypotheses are independent, but related: either the hallucination was caused by the phantasy diseased by some disorder like melancholic adustion; or the specter was the work of the demon. Thus, in the first case a well defined awareness existed that the mind could be a natural cause of illusion, while in the second, the source was regarded as supernatural. These last two explanations, as was demonstrated above, were often united. The *Malleus,* for example, makes it quite clear that the regent of the underworld can indeed cause apparitions which are not imaginary "...they [the doctors] all agree, that there are wizards and sorcerers who by the power of the devil can produce real and extraordinary effects, and these effects are not imaginary, and God permits this to be." (*Malleus*, 4.) [9] One need read only Mira de Amescua's *El esclavo del demonio* to ascertain the extent of the belief that the devil could conjure up illusions and artificial realities in order to deceive his prey. [10]

It was considerably more probable, however, that Satan or his accomplices, would first attempt to overthrow reason by some means before invoking the supernatural, because theoretically, the healthy individual, sound in his virtue and fortified by an uncompromised rational faculty, would recognize immediately the unnatural composition of Lucifer's arts. And once the diabolical plan had been revealed, all the demons in hell were powerless to perpetrate further deception as long as the hunted called upon the name of the Lord for protection. Thus with reason and judgement intact, only an act of volition, involving a pact with the eternal enemy of Christ, could insure a triumph for Heaven's pariah. So it was that Lucifer and his allies became masters of the art of subtlety, persuasion, counterfeit appearances, disguise, and subterfuge, because victory depended primarily on seducing reason so as to lead the lamb into darkness where right and wrong were necessarily more difficult to differentiate. The tractates concerned with witchcraft and demonology, as well as those dealing with death, take special care to point out that acute illness and the twilight consciousness that precedes departure from life are times of gravest peril: it is then that the rational mind, delirious and ravaged by disease and fright, is most susceptible to the infernal machination. [11]

---

[9] Cf. also the following: "It is a most certain and most Catholic opinion that there are sorcerers and witches who by the help of the devil, on account of a compact which they have made with him, are able, since God allows this, to produce real and actual evils and harm, which does not render it unlikely that they can also bring about visionary and phantastical illusions by some extraordinary and peculiar means." (*Malleus*, 6.)

[10] Gaspar Navarro affirms that the demon, with his prodigious knowledge of the secret nature of all things, is capable of producing forms and likenesses from the earth and air: "Y assí si succediere que aparecen muertos, no son ellos, ni sus almas, sino ilusiones y fantasías de aquellos que el demonio dize que son, formando los cuerpos de vapores elementales y tierra, poniéndolos como astuto artífice sus colores y facciones." (*Tribunal*, 19r.)

[11] See, for example, the chapter of Alexo Venegas on this dangerous period between life and death in his *Tránsito*, NBAE, XVI, 169-173.

ACT III 145

Unnatural phenomena, therefore, could indicate God's intervention in the affairs of men, the 'materializations' of an atrabilious syndrome, the work of Satan, or a conjunction of the last two hypotheses. How, then, was the poor individual who suffered such an experience to distinguish between Christ and anti-Christ? Direct divine action was always a distinct possibility, but the appearances of phantoms, specters, and voices in the night were more probably the deceits of Lucifer and his legions. Apart from the generalized awareness of the devil's omnipresence, however, there did exist an even more specific criterion for determining whether or not a supernatural occurrence was diabolical or Providential. Gaspar Navarro declares that the demon's presence is known by the terrifying emotional impact it produces: "No solo no dexa buenos efetos, sino que antes dexa malos: ...causa también inquietud, que no se sabe entender de adonde viene, sino que parece resiste el alma, y se alvoreta [sic], sin saber de qué." (*Tribunal*, 32r.) Pedro Mercado alleges that God's voice produces a feeling of calm and inner tranquility, while Satan's disturbs and disquiets the soul: "En esto se da a entender quando Dios viene, y quando las cosas son suyas, ay suauidad, y no ay temores... quiero dezir, que si del ruydo que sienten quando le hablan quedan inquietos, y temerosos, es señal que aquel ruydo, y vozes son del demonio." (*Diálogos*, 40v.) [12]

The object of the foregoing discussion has been to provide a background perspective from which to analyze Lope's artistic creation of the ghost and the *labrador*. The hero's foreboding clairvoyance, together with his great sadness and fear, offer ample

---

[12] In France, the Protestant Louis Lavater writes: "Moreover popishe writers teach us to discerne good spirits from euill by foure meanes. First they say that if he be a good spirit, he will at the beginning, somewhat terrifie men, but againe soone reuiue and comforte them... Their second note is to discry them by their outward and visible shape. For if they appeare under the forme of a...blake ghoste, it may easily be gathered that it is an euill spirit. And that on the other side good spirits do appear vnder the shape of a doue, a man, a lambe, or in the brightnesse, and clere light of the sunn. We must also consider whether the voice whiche we heare be sweete, lowly, sober, sorowfull, or otherwise terrible and full of reproch, so they terme it." (Lewes Lavater, *Of Ghostes and Spirites Walking by Nyght*, trans. R. H. [London, 1572], facsimile edition by J. Dover Wilson and May Yardley [Oxford, England, 1929], 108.)

evidence of the melancholic complexion of his mind at this time. The stage directions concerning the ghost are of major importance here: "Al entrar don Alonso, una sombra con una máscara negra y sombrero." The black attire, especially the mask, would indicate that the *Fénix* intended for this phantom to represent a demoniacal phenomenon. The messages which the two deliver can hardly be said to soothe the young man's fears and anxieties. Likewise, the physical posture of the ghost, "puesta la mano en el puño de la espada," produces an attack of near hysteria in the hero's behavior, to such a degree, in fact, that he disavows his own identity when the specter beckons and utters his name: "No es posible. / Mas otro será, que yo / soy don Arturo Manrique." (819-b.) Terrified momentarily, Alonso then tries to rationalize his experience. First he says that the ghost is his own *sombra* (819-b.); from this he elaborates still another explanation — that what he saw was nothing more than "la fuerza de la tristeza, / la imaginación de un triste." (819-b.) To fear without cause, he affirms, "es de sujetos humildes." (819-b.) This much of his diagnosis derives from seventeenth-century medical lore. Or, groping for another rationale, was it "embustes de Fabia" (819-b.), who, in her 'kindly way,' was trying to warn him not to return to Olmedo by night for fear of the envy he had aroused in the townspeople?[13] Rodrigo, he argues, surely cannot be the reason for Fabia's admonition. (819-b.) What is of major interest here is that Alonso expresses his hypotheses as independent alternatives: *either* the specter corresponds to the fantasies of a depressed imagination, *or* it was sent by Fabia as a precaution. True to the prevailing pattern of representative irony, Alonso cannot grasp the interrelatedness of his thoughts, each of which communicates a fragment of the whole truth. Clearly, the young man walks alone in darkest solitude, both physically and metaphorically, as he has throughout the tragedy, deprived of reason's beacon. The healthy individual would have known that the vision was *aut Dei aut diaboli* by the nature of the

---

[13] The remark is peculiar for several reasons. Alonso still does not designate the source of this envy, saying only, "la envidia me sigue." (819-b.) Moreover, it has been Tello alone who has warned of Rodrigo's suspicions, not Fabia. From whence, therefore, does this envy emanate? Characteristically, Alonso has no answer.

feeling accompanying the experience. In the latter case, Navarro advises the victim to commend his soul to God, examine his conscience, and look to "el estado en que está." (*Tribunal*, 23v.) Only one whose reason slept would not have entrusted his safety to God.[14]

It is very difficult to affirm categorically whether the *sombra* and the *labrador* are to be regarded as the products of a frenzied mind ravaged by disease, or real spirits either sent or conjured by Fabia 'out of air and earth.' Lope leaves these phenomena surrounded in an atmosphere of mystery. In support of the latter view it should be pointed out that the evil spirits were believed more likely to appear at night, especially before midnight. Pierre Le Loyer states that they are most prone to "haunt all places, yet so it is that they have particularly affected some places, as crossroads, sepulchres, forests, deserts, etc."[15] Metaphorically, of course, Alonso has arrived at the crossroad of decision to turn back or not. The *labrador* warns: "Volved atrás, no paséis deste arroyo." (821-a.) Shortly thereafter Alonso says: "A la mitad dél [el camino] estoy..." (821-b.) Whether Lope intended the specters to be understood as black spirits arising from within, or summoned by Fabia from below is, in the last reckoning, of little importance. Learned and popular opinion on this matter was divided in the period. To be sure, there were those in the playhouses who could have made a good case for both hypotheses. What is of significance is that either point of view involves Fabia. It is in the effect of these visitations on the young man that their diabolical origin can be most concretely demonstrated, for the ghost intensifies the seizure of fear and confusion hitherto unknown in the valiant spirit of the Knight of Olmedo. With the arrival of the *labrador*, Alonso is so thoroughly demoralized and terrified that he *voluntarily* seeks

---

[14] An interesting comparison presents itself here. Alonso is not the only character in the play to experience a confrontation with the occult. We recall that in Act II, Tello, who *is* sane, relates his ghoulish mission with Fabia. When the hanging corpse spoke, the lackey was painfully aware of a disturbed natural order. The comparison of the reactions of both men to the supernatural emphasizes the clearness of mind in the one and the utter mental obfuscation of the other.

[15] Quoted from May Yardley's essay, "The Catholic Position in the Ghost Controversy of the Sixteenth Century," in Lavater, *Of Ghostes*, 235.

the company of others whom he offers to pay if they will only allow him to join their number. (821-b.) They, of course, he soon learns, are none other than Rodrigo and his men. Thus it can be said that Alonso's great fear, brought on by the phantoms, delivers him to his own executioners.

As if the supernatural appearances and the melancholic condition of the protagonist were not enough to reveal a pattern of connection between what happens and Fabia's identity as a witch, Lope has imprinted her image even more deeply into the texture of this action. Alonso gives clear indication that he realizes his pander is capable of some kind of unnatural communication when he exclaims, on seeing the *sombra*, "O embustes de Fabia son..." (819-b.) At this critical point, then, the dramatist does not lose the opportunity to mention the name of the *medianera*. Again he injects her image into the dialogue when the *labrador* states that he has heard his doleful ballad from a certain Fabia, and then darkly hints that it was she who sent him on his way to deliver its sad message. (821-a.) More striking, however, is the disposition of scenes set up by the playwright. It is highly revealing that the appearance of the *labrador* does not immediately follow that of the specter. Interposed between these two moments is an interstitial scene that diverts our attention momentarily from Alonso's eery experience to Rodrigo's arrival. This interruption repeats patterns seen elsewhere in Lope's technique and has several objectives. Rodrigo is furious, having learned of the "devoción fingida" (820-a.) and of the secret love affair. What is curious here is that he never explains how he fell heir to this information. His timely — or rather, untimely — interception of the hero poses still another question: what mediation guided him so unerringly to this sinister place precisely at this fateful moment? He had previously mentioned, having been humiliated in the ring, that *if* he found the *hidalguillo loco* between Medina and Olmedo he would change Inés's laughter into lament. (817-a.) This seemingly coincidental meeting recalls a similar rendezvous at the *reja* in the first *jornada*, which produced the ribbon incident. In both cases, the anti-hero appears at a crucial moment as if directed by some hidden intelligence to this locale at a specific time. Nor does he have to seek out his tormentor in the inky darkness, but rather his victim comes to him.

ACT III   149

Technically, the juxtaposition of scenes provides the audience with the knowledge that Rodrigo is present and, through him, Fabia.

If the *peripetia* represents that segment of tragedy in which all prior commitments and relationships are drawn into an organic unity and thus clarified, then Rodrigo's description now of Alonso's entrepreneur (quoted above, p. 77) is a remarkable structural achievement. These lines, so powerfully spoken by the antagonist, are, perhaps, the most important in the play. Lope has previously furnished his audience with periodic glimpses into the other reality behind the love duet, either through the eyes of Tello, or as it is reflected by Fabia herself. This particular portrait is, therefore, highly meaningful in that it comes from another character in the drama, one who has no hesitation to speak the truth for fear of irritating his master. By means of Rodrigo's enraged expostulation, Lope once again intrudes the now fully revealed identity of Fabia into the tragic reversal in making her the party to whom the catastrophic outcome of such a fair love must be charged. This same Fabia who can "move mountains, detain rivers, receives the obedience of all her vassals in hell, and can carry a man through the air to any of the four corners of the earth," must certainly be capable of subtle deception and supernatural manipulation, for such is the art of the necromancer. Fernando's comment serves to validate his comrade's appraisal: "Por la misma razón yo no tratara / de más venganza." (820-a.) Lope has thus organized the *peripetia* into a tryptich consisting of the *sombra*, the arrival of Rodrigo with his engraving of Fabia, and the *labrador,* in such a way that the middle 'panel' provides an explanation of the other two that surround it.

A question naturally arises at this juncture: what is the nature of Fabia's motivation in bringing about the death of the young Knight? The query is significant because its answer relates Fabia to the metaphysical implications of tragic irony and opens the way to an understanding of Alonso's stature as a representative hero. Renaissance witch treatises and trial accounts record numerous cases in which individuals willingly abjured the faith of their fathers in favor of the black theology after extensive persuasion by some malefactor or the devil himself. And if conversion were not possible, it was believed that Lucifer's ends had still been served when some poor victim could be enticed into sin, or better yet, that his fall into sin should lead to his murder by one of his own kind. The strategy, theoretically, was that if the prey should die because of his transgressions without the benefit of the holy ministrations, then perhaps the soul might become, as Lavater expounds, another demon of Lucifer's kingdom:

> Herevnto apperteine those words whiche we reade in S. Chrisostome's second sermon *De Lazara*. There he sheweth that many simple men haue bin in this erroure, that they haue thought the soules of those which were slayne by some violent death did become Diuels. He says further that the Diuel hathe persuaded many witches, and such as serue him being in this erroure, that they shoulde kill the tĕder bodies of many yong men, hoping they shold become Diuels, and do them seruice. (*Of Ghostes*, 173.)

Fabia's motivation, therefore, is consistent with that of the lord to whom she makes her genuflexion: to blaspheme the Maker and demonstrate Satan's reality, as the devil in *El esclavo del demonio* explains to Gil: "Heridas tengo, y por vengarme de ellas / coger no puedo a Dios porque está en su trono, / y me vengo en el hombre que es su imagen." [16]

As executor of the devil, the clever witch usually found that deception with the truth was her most potent weapon. "The diuell sometimes vttereth yͤ truth, that his words may haue the more credite, and that he may the more easely beguile them," writes Lavater. (*Of Ghostes*, 173.) The effectiveness of the *engaño con la verdad* explains why the ghost and the *labrador*, in the reversal, quite patently set before the hero's senses the vision of his own death. For the center of Alonso's tragic plight has been all along that he could not see the truth, that truth itself had become a veil of deception. Passion, it must be remembered, is a disease of the will that produces an overthrow of reason. And will is a blind faculty, as Covarrubias records. (*Tesoro*, 1012.) Stated in another way, then, Fabia knows that once Alonso commits himself to the dance of love he cannot turn back. By the same token, therefore, he will not flinch in the bullring, nor will he retreat from the

---

[16] Mira de Amescua, *El esclavo del demonio*, in Alpern and Martel, *Diez comedias*, 496.

ACT III   151

ghost, however true its message. It is interesting to observe that one of the hero's hypotheses to explain his confrontation follows precisely this reasoning: "O embustes de Fabia son, / que pretenden persuadirme / porque no me vaya a Olmedo, / *sabiendo que es imposible.*" (819-b, italics mine.) As if to underline dramatically just how blind Alonso is at this time, Lope ends the scene with the protagonist's exculpation of Rodrigo on the grounds of personal honor (819-b.), and begins the next with the arrival of the now frenzied anti-hero who gives the lie to the protagonist's still echoing words. The fact, therefore, that Fabia's messengers warn the young man is consistent with the structural integrity of the tragedy from its inception.

The tragic reversal is a culmination of events through which the dramatic artist reveals an order in nature seen as ironic or dualistic. As Lope reflects it in this tragedy, the cosmos is constituted according to an internal design which assumes an antithetical polarity of metaphysical-theological forces. In a word, the world is held together by the tension that this balance of opposites generates. Tragedy, for Lope, represents the unique art form that deciphers a master blueprint for man who is himself only one element of creation precariously suspended in the universal tension. Man's central dilemma is one of grasping the primitive complexity of nature's composition which links life to death, love to hate, light to darkness, and error to redemption. It is this articulation of the conjunction of opposites that the great tragedians seek to capture. Man, as portrayed in the figure of the hero, is placed in the position of a participator in nature, fundamentally capable of knowing its mysteries, yet, because of his own constitution, limited in his vision of reality. The more he strives to achieve happiness, enlightenment, fulfillment, or whatever it is that he seeks, the more he falls into the trap of deception that nature provides. Characteristically, he interprets the hieroglyphs wrongly, that is to say, in only one translation, totally unaware that in each cipher there is contained the same basic ambivalence that informs nature itself. The *peripetia*, then, is that final segment of the tragic action that reveals to the hero the extent of his misreading and produces an act of realization or *anagnorisis* on his part. It is because of the reversal that he comes at last to understand the profoundly deceptive irony in nature as expressed in his own destiny. The insight he gains into the relationship between *parecer* and *ser* denotes his transformation from an ordinary man to a representative tragic figure who acquires his new stature by virtue of this vital recognition. The *peripetia*, therefore, is the dramatic catalyst that distills the *anagnorisis*. But the price of such a precious vision of truth comes dearly indeed: for *la flor de Olmedo*, it amounts to life itself.

Alonso's recognition is peculiar in several respects. To begin with, it is exceedingly short in duration. Secondly, he makes no mention of Fabia. The brevity of his utterances at this point, of course, is due to the fact that he has been mortally wounded — shot — and is in the act of dying. Any prolonged discourse would run the risk of falling into the melodramatic which would be inconsistent with the solemnity of the moment. This, together with the urgency he feels to repair forthwith to his parents, is uppermost in his thoughts: "Tello, Tello, ya no es tiempo / más que de tratar del alma. / Ponme en tu caballo presto / y llévame a ver mis padres." (822-a.) The discourse that lays bare the moribund hero's understanding of his plight is set forth in ten lines which we shall examine carefully:

> ¡Qué poco crédito di
> a los avisos del cielo!
> Valor propio me ha engañado,
> y muerto envidias y celos.
> ¡Ay de mí! ¿Qué haré en un campo
> tan solo?
> ....
> ¡Dios mío, piedad! ¡Yo muero!
> Vos sabéis que fue mi amor
> dirigido a casamiento.
> ¡Ay Inés! (822-a.)

The most outstanding feature of these words is that Lope has combined the protagonist's statement of recognition with a confession that sheds further light on the *anagnorisis* itself, and is, thus, concordant with the hero's position as a Christian Knight of the Order of Alcántara.[17] In the few moments preceding his

---

[17] In Act II the Condestable asks the King to honor Alonso with the habit of the Order, a request the King is happy to grant. (811-a,b.) Ironically, the hero never learns of his appointment. As a member of the Order, of

death, what precisely does Alonso come to understand about his tragedy?

Uppermost in his mind is the categorical necessity to make his peace with God, and almost all that he says is subordinated to this urgency. In modifying the traditional recognition to a more Catholic *confessio*, Lope integrates the personal *anagnorisis* into a more comprehensive framework of redemption. The reasons for this alteration will be discussed shortly. More to the point at the moment is all that is assumed in his act of contrition and repentance. The fact that he calls upon his Maker for forgiveness *(piedad)*, carries with it profound meaning. His supplication for divine clemency indicates an entirely different consciousness in the hero in so far as it denotes a realization that his passionate interlude has been a deposition of God's Will, a turning away from the light. With death's first cold touch, he returns to the vital cognizance of God's presence, now supremely aware of his error and the need for forgiveness.

When the protagonist stood at Inés's window awaiting her arrival for the last time, he spoke briefly of marriage. The proof of his sincerity at that time is presented in the confession, for included in his remarks is the reminder to God that matrimony was always his objective. Now, this declaration of good intention further refines his tragic insight. It does in fact lie at the very heart of the irony which has resolved itself in his predicament. However 'right' the tragic hero's decisions and actions may seem to him, his solution to the problem at hand turns out to be wrong —*contraproducente*— thus emphasizing how fragile and limited man's judgement really is, especially so when he places such great confidence in his own rectitude and infallibility. To the enraptured lover, his passion appeared harmless and pure *because,* in his own words, it was "dirigido a casamiento." The remark reflects Alonso's realization that between honorable motive and personal conduct, between the ideal and the real, lies a metaphysical quagmire of deception and error into which the most well-meaning of men can become ensnared. Indeed, the greater the innocence, the greater

---

course, his duties would be to guard and protect against the Moors, or enemies of the Faith. Until the sixteenth century, all Knights were forbidden to marry.

the probability that they will stumble into one of the many traps. In the very act of turning to God, Alonso testifies to his recognition that love outside the Christian circumscription deprives the participant of his capacity to prevail over all the forces of destruction and mutability which such a love must spawn and to which it falls subject. It is only in his downfall that the tragic protagonist apprehends a hermeneutic vision into the underlying ambivalence of nature and himself. In the agony of death, Alonso at last sees that "fuera de Dios, todo se muda," as Lope has stated in his poem, "A la mudanza":

> No hay cosa humana fuerte,
> porque a todas alcanzas [la mudanza],
> la vida, toda en guerra convertida,
> milita hasta la muerte
> sujeta a mil mudanzas,
> y la muerte también se trueca en vida.
> Mal quedas definida,
> infinita mudanza,
> mas ya quedo contento;
> que tu conocimiento
> mudó mi antiguo error a la esperanza
> de un bien en que no hay duda,
> porque, fuera de Dios, todo se muda.[18]

Lope's apostrophe to *la mudanza* is a perfect description of the ironic mutability of nature as the tragic hero experiences it. Alonso's understanding of his own blindness is expressed in the lines: "Valor propio me ha engañado,/ y muerto envidias y celos." The word *valor*, of course, refers immediately to his obstinate refusal to turn back in the face of the supernatural confrontation. Yet it must be admitted that this same courage the hero displayed only a moment before is but another expression of the force that sustains the ardent flame of passion. In a word, passion's intoxicating ritual demands of its faithful a kind of willful courage not at all unlike the valor Alonso summoned in the *corrida,* or in the rendezvous with the phantoms. When he cries that his "valor propio" has

---

[18] In *Obras escogidas: Poesía y prosa,* ed. F. Sainz de Robles (Madrid, 1958), 104-a.

deceived him, he has, then, discovered another of the many ironies which inform the tragic view of nature and the paradoxical design of forbidden love. Courage, the sometimes wayward issue of *voluntas*, is the underground spring of life that nourishes love's blossom, but which, as the youthful protagonist now clearly verbalizes, also provides nurture for the thorns of *envidia* and *celos*.

We mentioned above that Alonso's *anagnorisis* is peculiar in that no mention is made here of Fabia's implication in the ironic ambivalence. Are we to assume from this that Lope intended Alonso's realization to be only partial? Such a facile explanation does not take into account that his remarks about the "embustes de Fabia" in the preceding scenes patently demonstrated his awareness of her skills. That he may have preferred to overlook her essentially occult background does not mean that he did not know her reputation. The reasons for the seeming absence of the go-between at this most vital time lie in the very nature of the recognition. However much Alonso may now comprehend *what* his sin has been, and *how* his world has entrapped him, these realizations are but a small fraction of the more comprehensive vision he gains in catastrophe: that insight has to do with God's plan itself, and the always vexatious problem of evil. If Satan was cast out of Heaven for his rebelliousness, then why was he not utterly destroyed by the Maker at the time of this historical event, which from the Christian point of view, must be considered the single most cataclysmic occurrence since the Creation. The answer lies in the fact that were it not for the *magisterium* of Lucifer subsequent to his dismissal, then, indeed, there would be no *mudanza*, no ironic order in nature, and consequently no conditions in which to cultivate a courtly deviation. The fall of man from Eden, and all the ensuing tragedies which that disaster brought, recapitulate in a monotonous crescendo the horrendous fissure that the fallen angel's insurrection opened in the primeval harmony. Likewise, from Eve's fateful dialogue with the serpent onward in time, Satan's malevolence has punctuated the chronicle of man's incompletion.

The very continuing existence of the devil, and all of his allies, testifies to a more comprehensive plan within the Divine Intelligence. The *Malleus* is most lucid on this point:

> The work of God can be destroyed by the work of the devil in accordance with what we are now saying with reference to the power and effects of witchcraft. *But since this can only be by the permission of God*, it does not at all follow that the devil is stronger than God. Again, he cannot use so much violence as he wishes to harm the works of God, because if he were unrestricted he would utterly destroy all the works of God. (*Malleus*, 11.)

Thus, to the authors of the *Hammer*, the proof of Providential Sufferance is obvious in the fact that "all the works of God" have not been demolished by the demon. God, rather, permits Lucifer a certain sphere of activity, for which He must have a supreme rationale. Fray Martín de Castañega, pondering the relationship between the witch and God's Will, affirms four reasons for the presence of Satan and his legions, which will help us to understand Alonso's remark: "¡Qué poco crédito di / a los avisos del cielo!"

> La primera, para confirmar la fe de los flacos porque muchos hay que son católicos en que no tienen error en su entendimiento, mas no tienen tan arraigadas algunas verdades católicas como ellos desean... La segunda es por manifestar la fe de los firmes y fundados en la fe... E como dice Sant Pablo: bien es que haya herejías, para que los firmes y aprobados sean conocidos. La tercera razón es que Dios permite estas cosas en pena de los obstinados... Destas resulta y se sigue la cuarta razón, y es por manifestar la bondad y grandeza suya; que no permitiría en el universo nacer males, si dende no se cogiesen muy mayores bienes.[19]

For Castañega, then, the devil becomes an instrument of God through which the Divine Existence is made more comprehensible to man. Gaspar Navarro is of the same opinion: "...lo permite Dios por nuestro bien, para que si acaso estamos en mal estado, y vivimos mal nos conozcamos y enmendemos." (*Tribunal*, 23.) Lavater writes, "...except God by these meanes [evil spirits] dyd cast feare uppon them [those who have strayed away], and as it

---

[19] Martín de Castañega, *Tratado de las supersticiones y hechicerías*, Bibliófilos Españoles, XVII, 31.

were with a snaffle or brydle, did hale and draw them backe."
(*Of Ghostes*, 187.) Burton, in discussing the ultimate reasons for
sickness, either natural or induced by Satan's representatives,
agrees with Lavater that these calamities serve to create a greater
awareness of God:

> Or else these chastisements are inflicted upon us for our
> humiliation, to exercise and try our patience here in this
> life, to bring us home, to make us to know God oursel-
> ves... *In morbo recolligit se animus,* as Pliny well per-
> ceived... (*Anatomy*, I, 132.)

Thus, in temptation, sickness, heresy, deviation from orthodoxy, in
witchcraft and demonolatry there is a purpose, and that objective is
to make mortals conscious of God's majesty and paternity. For
how did Eve and her mate come to know the full meaning of the
Lord's protection until they were seduced into error by the serpent?

Alonso's *anagnorisis* is complete, therefore, in that it expresses
this reconciliation between Fabia's powers and Providential Char-
ity. For in the view of witchcraft current in the seventeenth
century and earlier, the consciousness of God's accessibility and
man's dependency on Him was made firm and urgent through
the devil's minions. This was their mission, this was why God
suffered them to exist along with their sovereign. Thus any dominion over the inner secrets of the natural order, whether the power
to visit inflictions or create "blacke formes" out of the night air,
ultimately served the Supreme Intelligence as an efficient channel
of comunication through which to "hale and draw back" those
who stood in need of correction. Lavater, in expounding this
subtle, yet profoundly essential, relationship between evil and
recognition, quotes Paul:

> For in the second Epistle to the Corinth. and xii. chap.
> Paul sayth: And lest I shold be exalted out of measure,
> through the excellencie of reuelatiõ, ther was giuen vnto
> mee unquietnesse through the fleshe, euen the messanger
> of Satan to buffet me, bicause I should not be exalted
> out of measure. For this thing besought I the Lord thrice,
> that it mighte depart fro me. And he sayd vnto me: My
> grace is sufficiĕt for thee, for my strength is made perfect
> through weakenesse. Except God did shvt up the waye
> before vs with certaine stops and lets, we shold not know

our selues, we shoulde not vnderstande whereof we stand in need. (*Of Ghostes*, 176.)

Lucifer, as his name would indicate, therefore, does indeed still play the role of the "light bearer' in that through his franchise —*Dei permissu*— the eternal light shines all the more brilliantly because it has ordained a field of opposed and contrasting darkness within which it may be seen. Thus has God arranged the metaphysical mechanism of perception with which man is enabled to distinguish redemption from damnation. Justina of *El mágico prodigioso*, like Alonso assailed by the devil, exclaims: "Algún hechizo mortal/ se está haciendo contra mí,/ y fuera el conjuro tal,/ que a no haver Dios, desde aquí/ me dejara ir tras mi mal./ Mas Él me ha de defender,/ y no sólo del poder/ desta tirana violencia;/ pero mi humilde inocencia/ no ha de dejar padecer." [20] The mention of her remark here serves to elucidate Alonso's realization by contrast. Whereas she is aware that her melancholy hallucinations are the work of the demon, she is no less cognizant that an appeal to God will preserve her innocence from the machinations of the black prince. But, "if there were no God," she says, surely she would let herself follow the infernal path. Calderón's heroine, then, already possesses the truth that Alonso discovers in his catastrophe, namely that without God, Lucifer's kingdom is infinite and variable ("fuera de Dios, todo se muda"), but that exposure to the diabolical deception, which is man's lot, awakens the need for, and consequently the indwelling consciousness of God's Grace. Gil, the anchorite of *El esclavo del demonio*, and Cipriano of *El mágico prodigioso*, in a way not too dissimilar from Alonso's, achieve this understanding after having fallen into the devil's trap. The Knight's *anagnorisis*, in the last analysis, is a many sided experience. It is first a recognition of the ironic complexion of nature and of his own blindness. It is a confession of error that reveals an awareness of the distinction between the ideal and the real. But, most importantly, it is a clairvoyant reconciliation of the two halves of the metaphysical irony into a single supra-consciousness of God's design and a resultant return to the bosom of orthodoxy. Lope has

---

[20] In Pedro Calderón de la Barca, *Obras completas: Dramas*, ed. Luis Astrana Marín (Madrid, 1945), 1076-a.

dramatically accommodated the hero's enlightenment and homecoming to an action mode that literally places the young man in an act of return to his parents to assure them of his well-being. Symbologically, therefore, the moment of his recognition is represented as a homecoming to the place of his birth, and spiritually —in calamity— a return to the Father and to the Church by analogy.

It is essential to Lope's conception to understand at this time that in death and the final clairvoyance which accompanies it, the hero attains true tragic proportions as a representative man in a distinctly Christian perspective. For Alonso is vouchsafed an insight into the 'tragic sense of life' available to all men yet experienced by few. The very fact that he comprehends the tragic *mysterium* attests to his position as a selected individual, one chosen by God as a symbolic exemplar of His Inscrutable Will. As Pedro Mercado reminds his reader, those most assailed by Satan's treachery through the evil agency of a witch or other intermediary, suffer their afflictions because they enjoy divine favor and sympathy:

> Y más digo, que aun tentar ni ocasionarnos no podría [the devil]: sino fuesse para mayor merecimiento y gloria nuestra. Y no se alcança un estado, lleno de tan perfectos bienes, sino por trabajos y tentaciones. Y no se halla hombre, que Dios amasse, al qual no probasse con ellos: conformando siempre la tentación con el tentado, y dándole favor para vencerla. Y los santos bienaventurados tienen por mayor tentación, no ser tentados... que ninguna persona le parecía a él [Demetrio, one of the characters of the dialogue] más desventurada, que a quien ninguna desventura le avía acaescido, en toda su vida: porque el tal hombre, o a si mismo no se conocía: pues nunca se avía probado, o estava aborrecido de Dios: pues nunca se avía acordado de él para probarlo. (*Diálogos*, 156r.)

Within this doctrine of the necessity of Lucifer's works as a priority to "mayor merecimiento y gloria" is contained, of course, a double exculpation of Alonso's departure from righteousness. First, there is the clear implication that he should not be held entirely reprehensible for his sins because of the great powers vested in Fabia, although it cannot be denied that he invited his own misfortunes. Her identity, however, diminishes the youthful hero's transgressions. Even Lavater admits that witches prey on "the tēder bodies of many yong men." Likewise, in the degree of success she enjoys in deceiving the lovers, their young innocence is proclaimed. More significantly, however, is Mercado's explanation of diabolical intervention as an indication of God's interest and purpose. Here is set forth Lope's adjustment of tragic fate or destiny to a Christian reference: if Alonso succumbs, it is because God's Will is fulfilled. But he does not die meaninglessly, and this is why the dramatist takes care to give the hero a proper Christian *anagnorisis*. By the end of the tragedy, he emerges as that peculiar individual described by Aristotle, neither a saint, nor an ordinary man. He becomes, rather, a symbol of the Christian view of life as temptation and redemption, of 'aconsciousness' and supraconsciousness. That he does fall into error and transgression assures his humanity; that he comes to recognize his mistake and turns to God, makes him worthy of the habit of Alcántara with its green cross of hope awarded him earlier in the play by the king.

It should now be clear that Lope has exquisitely converted courtly protocol into a Christian tragedy. Let us review the principal specifics of this accommodation. The courtly lover seeks a transformation in love, a release from earthly routine into a condition of higher knowledge and virtue. We have seen how Alonso's clandestine adventure has led him ineluctably to a new life, a Christian release in death, and a redemptive recognition that is his final *guerdon*. Lope's dramatic usage of the courtly paradox — life is death and death is life — is abundantly apparent in the resolution of the tragedy. Indeed, Alonso's life has been a steady dying, and in death he achieves the eternal life and fame so ardently pursued by the classical courtly aspirant. Tello terminates his lengthy funeral announcement and oration with a reminder that the glory of the Caballero de Olmedo shall never perish: "...cuyo entierro/ será el del fénix; señor,/ después de muerto viviendo/ en las lenguas de la fama,/ a quien conservan respeto." (824-b.) Above all, the courtly lover must suffer, because it is in affliction that his salvation is formed. Valency comments: "Torn in this manner, the lover was seldom well; no earthly *guerdon* could appease his torment. But his illness was the promise of his salvation, and the nobility of the gentle heart was revealed precisely in this spiritual malaise which set off love's elect from the rest of mankind." (*In*

Praise, 252.) Alonso's passion is at once his torment, the cause of his death, and the way that leads to Christian enlightenment.

* * *

Fortunately for the present investigator, all that has been said above concerning the nature of Alonso's *anagnorisis* and the doctrine of redemption through temptation, suffering, and the reign of Lucifer in the affairs of men, has been abstracted by Lope for us in two little known pieces: *El auto del Pan y del Palo* (in RAE, II, 229-241.), and *El auto de los cantares* (*Ibid.*, 407-417.) These two works might be no more than dramatic curiosities were it not for the very cogent fact that they are related to the tragedy by the surviving *estribillo* of the Caballero legend. In both the dramatist has introduced slight modifications to adjust the poetry of the refrain to Christ. In the *Auto del Pan y del Palo*, Regocijo, speaking to Buen Año of Jesús, describes the Son of God in the following lines:

>   No tuvo ni ha de tener
>   Más de treinta y tres, que luego
>   Que los cumplió le mataron.
>   ¿No has oído aquellos versos:
>   Que de noche le mataron
>   Al divino Caballero,
>   Que era la gala del Padre
>   Y la flor de tierra y cielo? (RAE, II, 230-b.)

In the *Auto de los cantares* the lines read:

>   Que de noche le mataron
>   Al Caballero,
>   A la gala de María
>   La flor del cielo.
>   Como el sol que arde
>   Tanto se encubría,
>   Noche parecía
>   Aunque era la tarde.
>   La muerte cobarde
>   Mató, aunque ella ha muerto,
>   Al Caballero,
>   A la gala de María,
>   La flor del cielo. (RAE, II, 411-b.)

Quite evidently Lope saw in the tale of the Knight of Olmedo or at least in his reconstitution of it, a symbolic representation of Christ's passion, and the communication which that passion was intended to convey to mankind.[21] The following discussion will examine briefly the first of the two *autos* since its exposition is more pertinent to the tragedy and is the more complete of the two. The Rey Eterno has just married the Esposa and, as the *auto* begins, we witness a wedding celebration. The Esposa is clothed in elaborate and radiant robes. She retires to the nuptial chamber (*el altar*) to prepare herself for the consummation of the marriage. At this point, the Rey Eterno summons Cuidado and delivers the following message:

>   Si aquí
> Viniere mi Esposa ahora,
> No como a Esposa y Señora
> Que habéis servido por mi,
> La tratéis de aquí adelante,
> Sino con mucha aspereza:
> Desnudadle la riqueza,
> No la del alma importante,
>   Sino sola la exterior,
> Que la interior sóla ella
> Puede aumentalla o perdella. (234-b.)

Cuidado, who, by the way, is presented as the servant of the King, is shocked at this command. The King then explains that in all of this there is a mystery: "Tiene misterio esta prueba:/ Cuando era en principios nueva,/ La daba Pan celestial;/ Tratábala con regalo;/ Pero ya que sabe amarme,/ Por mi Cruz vaya a buscarme;/ Sepa del Pan y del Palo." (234-b.) The mystery of which the King speaks is, of course, the redemptive cause and effect relationship between the symbolic *Pan* and *Palo*, grace and suffering. Cuidado explains that the Señor Eterno expresses his love through the visitation of suffering on the body and spirit of the beloved:

---

[21] I do not know the respective dates of the two *autos*. If they were written after the tragedy, then it can be inferred that Lope has allegorized the substance of the longer play. If before, it would seem that the *Caballero* dramatizes the doctrine put forth in the *autos*.

ACT III

> Extraños amores son
> Los de este Señor Eterno;
> Cuando más dulce y más tierno,
> Cuando más afición,
>   Entonces más riguroso;
> Mas bien se deja entender,
> Que consiste en padecer
> Todo el amor del Esposo.
>   El llama con su regalo,
> Y con su pan, mas después
> Quiere, pues su Cruz lo es
> Que haya del Pan y del Palo. (234-b.)

The exegesis of Cuidado is vital to the understanding of the *Caballero de Olmedo* and its architecture. In the *auto* the King expresses his attraction to, and love for, the Esposa prior to his announcement of the trial by temptation. What follows, therefore, is but another manifestation of his divine attraction. Falsedad explains: "Tal vez en castigos viene / Del mismo Dios el regalo." (236-a.) Falsedad and his fellow tormentor, Persecución, then assail the bride, accuse her of adultery and attempt to extort a willing denunciation from her of the Esposo. She, now divested of her magnificent attire and clothed in "ropa de sayal" and a "silicio," laments and wonders about the sudden change in fortune, this rapid *peripetia* which has transformed *bodas* into *tragedias*. El Niño Jesús appears and explains what has happened and why. Of interest is the Esposa's innocent remark: "Pensaba yo que ser vuestra / Me reservaba de ver Persecuciones" (237-b.), which is also Alonso's tragic miscalculation. Jesús proceeds to reveal to the grief-stricken bride the rationale for her present status, a discourse which is highly reminiscent of Alonso's plight:

> Regalos mi amor os muestra,
> No los tengáis por menores,
> Si os doy aquestos castigos,
> Porque yo a los más amigos
> Los doy por grandes favores.
>   *Cuando quito la salud,*
> los hijos, la hazienda, el gusto,
> *Doy el pleito y el disgusto*
> *El agravio, la inquietud.* (237-b, italics mine.)

And all of these afflictions, he affirms, are "palos de esta cruz." (238-a.) The way to *Pan*, then, requires first the heavy load which the *Palo* imposes. "Por este Palo, mi Esposa, / Se ha de subir a mi Pan, / Porque sin Cruz no le dan." (238-b.) Finally, Buen Año comments that none of these torments decreed by God can be effective if there is a lack of good conscience: "Porque no le [placer] puede haber / Adonde hay mala consciencia." (239-b.) To those who have not truly turned away from the Divine Presence there shall be revealed the secret of the mystery inherent in the symbolism of *Pan y Palo*, which both the Esposa ("Aquella cruz me dejó / Para que alcanzase el Pan" [239-b.]), and Alonso share.

In the *Auto de los cantares*, Lope utilizes very much the same allegorical characters. The modifications which he introduces here warrant some examination. The Esposa represents the Church, who is courted by the Esposo or Christ. But Jesús has an antagonist, Lucifer, who in this piece is called the Competidor. His interest in the Esposa, like that of the witches in their victims, is not for love of the fair lady as such, but is, rather, intended as an insult to the Esposo: "No la quiero por querella / Tanto como por quitalla / Al que ha venido por ella." (407-a.) He is fully aware, however, that the Bride would not receive him in his natural form and physiognomy. Envidia, his constant companion, advises him to disguise himself in the same attire as that worn by the Esposo: "¿Cristo no viene galán / Con esa capa encarnada / Y el velo del blanco Pan? / Pues toma alguna imitado / De las penas que te dan." (408-a.) To which Competidor replies: "Bien dices: fingirme quiero / Angel de Luz, y a la Esposa / Decir que por ella muero." (408-a.) The great emphasis placed on articles of clothing in both pieces, especially the second, recalls Fabia's many faces and camouflages. The *autos*, therefore, fundamentally agree with the thought of those who pondered the problem of *maleficium* and its relationship to the Providential plan. If God's Grace is made manifest in temptation, error, and suffering, then Cuidado, Envidia, Persecución, Competidor, and Fabia become, in this framework, integral functioning elements in His design, independent in their respective roles, yet subordinate to His autonomy. And passion, too, because it exists, is no less an agent in the Providential revelation. It is Tello who points out that passion is at once Alonso's suffering and the path that leads to his redemption: "La noche de aquellas fiestas / que a la Cruz de Mayo hicieron /

caballeros de Medina, / para que fuese tan cierto / que donde hay cruz hay pasión..." (824-a.) It is in the ambivalence of the word *pasión* (*passio*, suffering, and an erotic attraction) that Lope's conception of the tragic hero as a homologue of Christ can be seen. As Christ's love resulted in His Crucifixion, so Alonso's passion has brought about his death. There are indeed many parallel reminiscences between the Caballero and Jesus which merit an examination because they bear on the transfiguration of the hero.

The delicate congruency of Christ and *la flor de Olmedo* is perhaps partially inherent in the nature of tragedy whose protagonist is born to fulfill a destiny, an ironic fate, that renders his life and sufferings symbolic. As such he stands midway between the ordinary and the divine, partaking of both categories as finite in his humanity, infinite in his spiritual potential. In short, he has a mission to realize on earth which is analogous to that of the sacrificial victim who is proffered to the gods. Lope's tragedy makes it clear that his understanding of the Knight of Olmedo is that of the individual who was born to die, and in whose death the collective sins and glories of mankind are reflected. This is the first reminiscence between Christ and Alonso. Their deaths become symbolic triumphs over the very forces that effected their convictions. In murdering his competitor, Rodrigo achieves that which he set out to undo: the passion of the lovers is assured an eternal dimension because of the distance and separation which death assures. And those who conspired against Jesus likewise made themselves into the instrument of His Ascension and therefore guaranteed His glory.

It is perhaps at the time of Alonso's death that Lope most clearly insinuates the image of Christ into the configuration of his hero. In an earlier discussion we pointed out that witches were believed to have been instructed to strike during the times of religious celebrations. Of all the *fiestas sagradas* available to him, Lope has selected the Cruz de Mayo celebration for its obvious association with the Crucifixion and the symbol of the Cross. The death of the Son, according to the Gospels, occurred during the Feast of the Passover, which commemorates the deliverance of the Israelites from their Egyptian overlords. Thus the Jews were destined to suffer bondage in order to achieve liberation and a fulfillment of their history up to that point. Now Jesus's death symbolizes the redemption of man from the flesh, that is to say, sin and darkness, through love. In the Crucifixion and subsequent Resurrection, God revealed the existence of the newborn spiritual self inherent in man's creation. The Passover recalls the deliverance from political servitude, and Easter, the liberation from spiritual bondage. Both Jesus and Alonso were destined to die, then, at times of religious celebrations that commemorate a revealing of the Father's Will expressed as an act of emancipation. But what is significant in this coincidence of events and times is that the background celebrations constitute the greater light which is reflected in turn by the respective deaths. Alonso's demise, therefore, experienced within this time perspective, acquires a complementary coloration through analogy: as Christ bore His Cross — i.e., His Passion — because of His doctrine of love that had aroused the envy and enmity of the priests and Pharisees, so Alonso departs this life because of his love — his passion — which also had awakened the jealousy and hatred of Rodrigo. Thus Christ's Passion became synonymous with His love, and in the long journey toward Golgotha the interdependency of *Pan* and *Palo* was formulated. Similarly, Lope's hero arrives on this appointed day at a clairvoyant knowledge of the event it celebrates because the circumstances of his own fate recapitulate its drama and mystery of revelation through suffering, of rebirth through the spiritual purification which passion was supposed to render. For, above all, courtly passion was a suffering and, as such, it became a cross which all of love's elect had to bear in their search for higher being. Professor Soons, taking note of this symmetry of image which reflects the greater figure of Jesus through Alonso, writes: "Whatever end may be reserved for other men, the knight must, if he is called to do so, die in symbolic repetition of Christ's passion, the immolation of the natural man. This again reinforces the significance of the festival for Lope's play..." (*art. cit.*, 166.)

Thus far it has been shown that the timing of their respective deaths shares a common symbolic conception — that of liberation from bondage. The transformation of Jesus into the Savior and Alonso into the characteristic tragic hero is further seen in the 'programmed' nature of their lives. Christ appeared on earth with a mission to accomplish. His destiny was to bring a "new commandment," as we read in John 13: 34, 35. It is precisely in John's narrative that we find the strongest suggestion of a divinely determined fate for the Son. Time and again the Evangelist reports that "his hour was not yet come." And throughout all the Gospels Jesus seems to be fully conscious of His approaching death and its meaning for man. When the Savior had dipped the sop and given it to Judas Iscariot as a sign of His betrayor, John remarks: "Therefore, when he [Judas] was gone out, Jesus said, Now is the Son of Man glorified, and God is glorified in Him." (13: 31.) The refrain of the legend emphasizes the fact that the Caballero is destined also to die, and therefore, everything we witness in Lope's tragedy points toward that event in such a way that Alonso's life and love acquire an equally noticeable 'programmed' or scheduled character. Alonso's moments of clairvoyance remind one of Jesus's foretelling His own sacrifice. But herein lies the difference: whereas the Son of God knows He will soon rejoin the Father, Alonso, being mortal, cannot comprehend the meaning of his feelings, dreams, and visions.

John tells his reader that Jesus "was not of this world." He comes from without to deliver a new commandment, and in performing His commission, He incurred the wrath of the establishment which saw in the Nazarene a threat to the prevailing order. Alonso's passion, likewise, falls outside the prescribed code of social etiquette. And, similar to Christ, he comes from another place, thus making his destiny and origin poetically consonant. The result of the Redeemer's preaching was that the chief priests "took council against him," the same as Rodrigo eventually resolves to destroy his tormentor. The betrayal of the Lord by Judas, the Gospels affirm, was preceded by Satan's entry into the disciple's heart. In Lope's *peripetia* we find a strong suggestion that Fabia has betrayed the confidence of the two lovers, for how else would Rodrigo know about the charade ("la devoción fingida"), about the "cartas de romance traducido"? (820-a.) To be sure he could not have learned from Inés, Leonor, or Tello. And who else except these three *and Fabia* knew with certainty that Alonso would return to Olmedo this night? The suspicion of Fabia's duplicity comes to the surface when the *labrador* says that Fabia had sent him ("yo cumplí / con deciros la canción" [821-a.]), to sing a song in which mention is made of the *sombra* (821-a.) whose appearance has just taken place. Fabia, then, had to know that the ghost would materialize to announce the hero's death at the hands of Rodrigo. The same suspicion is further reinforced after the disaster when she tells Inés that an even greater evil awaits the maiden. (822-b.)

The Evangelists all associate the place of betrayal with the crossing of the brook Cedron. "And Judas also, which betrayed him, knew the place: for Jesus ofttimes resorted thither with his disciples," John writes. (18: 1,2.) A similar brook figures strongly in Alonso's ambush. The *labrador* warns: "...no paséis / deste arroyo." (821-a.) The brook becomes the point of rendezvous where Rodrigo overtakes Alonso. But Jesus did cross over, even knowing it would be in this locale that the authorities, led there by Judas, would apprehend Him. Nor can Lope's protagonist retreat one step from his scheduled fate at this foreordained place, for it is in the nature of the Messiah and the tragic hero that their lives correspond to a prefigured pattern. Thus, when we consider that Lope utilized the refrain in his *autos* to refer to Jesus, and then compare the design of Alonso's portrayal with the life of the Nazarene, one cannot escape the understanding that the dramatist fashioned his treatment of the Caballero legend so as to adjust the artifice of tragedy to the symbology of Christ's sojourn and death. In both external detail and doctrine there does indeed exist a deliberately blurred parallelism in both figures. Tragedy is, after all, descended from a religious ritual in which the spectator partakes of the mystery of life and death, incompletion and redemption, and the reconciliation of an ironic universe with the will of the Gods.

* * *

I shall dedicate a final discussion to certain symbols and imagery scattered throughout the tragedy which seem to corroborate my interpretation. In what is to follow I acknowledge my gratitude to Mrs. Alison Turner, one of my students, who first called my attention to the *jilguero* of the dream narration. Mrs. Turner is from Britain and is an amateur birdwatcher. The English translation usually stated for the *jilguero* is 'linnet.' The ordinary European linnet, however, Mrs. Turner pointed out, does not have the coloration of the bird in the dream. Alonso's *jilguero* is the goldfinch, common to England and Spain. The confusion arises in the fact that both the linnet and the goldfinch are members of the same family. In a study she wrote for me subsequently, she discovered that the goldfinch was a favorite symbol in Medieval and Renaissance painting, and a common housepet throughout Southern Europe during the period. This symbolic character of the goldfinch, in turn, suggested further investigation, the results of which will be presented in this section.

We shall begin, however, with the title of the play. The word *caballero* was frequently used to refer allegorically to Jesus and needs no further elucidation. The imagery associated with the name Olmedo, however, demands a careful scrutiny. 'Olmedo' resembles closely the word *olmeda* or elm grove, both being derived quite obviously from *olmo*. According to Fergusson, the elm alludes to the dignity of life. "Its all-encompassing growth and the spreading of its great branches in every direction symbolizes the strength which is derived by the devout from their faith in the Scriptures." [22] Gertrude Jobes gives approximately the same definition, but adds a significant new meaning: "Beauty, charm, stateliness, graciousness, dignity, courtly. Subject to disease. Christian symbol of strength." [23] Covarrubias writes of another aspect: "Especie de álamo, árbol conocido, del nombre latino *ulmus*. Es símbolo del que apoya a otro, que sin su favor no podía valer ni subir, como la parra que se abraça con él y sube hasta su cumbre." (*Tesoro*, 837-a.) The association of the elm with the vine was an exceedingly common one in the seventeenth century, especially in the Mediterranean countries. So much so in fact, that Shakespeare, Milton, and Browne allude to the natural affinity even though in England the vine was never trained to elms "in the Italian fashion." [24] It is in Pliny that we first read of this friendship which is so great that it is impossible to separate the two. [25]

---

[22] George Fergusson, *Signs and Symbols in Christian Art* (New York, 1954), 36.
[23] Gertrude Jobes, *A Dictionary of Mythology, Folklore, and Symbols* (New York, 1961), I, 506.
[24] Henry N. Ellacombe, *The Plant Lore and Garden Craft of Shakespeare* (London, 1884), 87.
[25] Caius Plinius, *The Natural History*, trans. J. Bostock and H. T. Riley (London, 1857), III, 370.

Interestingly, the Roman writer remarks that the form of the *quincunx* was the best for trees and shrubs intended to support the vine. The *quincunx* was a cross or two Roman v's set against one another at the apex of their angles. [26]

The vine, of course, expresses the relationship between God and man, and is a sign, therefore, of Christ. [27] Thus the image of the vine and the elm lent itself to a symbolism of constant, inseparable love. Vélez de Guevara employs it in *Reinar después de morir*. Inés tells the Príncipe: "Vi luego que de una vid / Un olmo galán se enlaza." (BAE, XLV, 113-b.) Vélez's metaphor is interesting in that the vine appears to be supporting the elm. García, of *Del rey abajo ninguno*, describes his love for Blanca as analogous to the marriage of the elm and the vine: "Las almas en nuestros brazos / vivan heridas y estrechas, / ya con repetidas flechas, / ya con recíprocos lazos; / no se tejan con abrazos / la vid y el olmo frondoso, / más estrechos que tu esposo / y tú, Blanca..." [28] This same notion of unending love lies, of course, at the very root of the image when the vine refers to Jesus.

Luis de Granada observes that the vine will flee a plant or tree that might be hostile to it:

> Mas las vides tienen sus ramales, que son como manos, con que se abrazan con los árboles, y suben a lo alto sobre hombros ajenos, y así también se apartan de algunas plantas que les son contrarias y dañosas... como de cosa pestífera... [29]

Elsewhere he expounds on the symbolism of the vine and the tree, explaining that they represent the image of redemption:

> Y porque aquí se hace mención de las viñas, no será razón pasar en silencio la fertilidad de las vides. Porque con ser la vid un árbol tan pequeño, no es pequeño el fruto que da... Y aunque este árbol sea tan pequeño, y no pueda por sí subir a lo alto, no le faltó remedio para eso, porque dél proceden unos ramilicos con los cuales se prende en las ramas de los árboles, y sube cuanto ellos

---

[26] *Ibid.*, III, 468.
[27] See, for example, Matthew 12:33, John 15:1.
[28] In Alpern and Martel, *Diez comedias*, 743.
[29] Luis de Granada, *Introducción del símbolo de la fe*, in *Obras*, ed. Fray Justo Cuervo (Madrid, 1908), V, 57.

> suben, especialmente cuando se juntan con árbol muy alto. En los cuales paresce estar expresa la imagen de nuestra redempción, porque desta manera subimos los hombres... arrimándonos a aquel alto cedro del monte Líbano, que es Cristo... (*Introducción*, V, 104.)

Fray Luis clearly relates the vine to the tree, each in need of the other, in their search for fertility, expanding the image in turn to include the doctrine of love, redemption, and the divine mission of Christ.

Covarrubias, in his definition of the elm, called it a species of poplar. The poplar tree is also related to the inherent symbology of the title of the tragedy. Don Sebastián explains that its leaves indicate a symbolism of time because they turn around immediately after the summer solstice:

> Por el álamo significavan el tiempo; conviene a saber el día y la noche, y los solsticios, porque se buelven las hojas. Háseme antojado, que por la semejança que tiene el álamo al olmo, assí en esta propiedad de volvérsele las hojas, como a ser infructífero y amar las riberas de los ríos ...ser escudero de honor y braçeros de la vid; los castellanos confundimos el nombre, y por la semejança que tiene el pópulo al olmo, le llamamos álamo... (*Tesoro*, 63-b.)

Juan Eduardo Cirlot calls the poplar a symbol for the tree of life: "Es así el árbol de la vida, verde del lado del agua y ennegrecido del lado del fuego." [30] The poplar, then, so often confused with the elm for their similar characteristics, displays a natural symbolism related to darkness and light, sun and earth. Thus the images of the poplar, the vine, and the elm appear to offer at least a partial explanation into the creative intuition of Lope in his drawing forth a symmetry between Christ and Alonso such that Alonso emerges as a selected man, one who supports the vine. It is interesting to note that toward the end of the *Auto de los cantares*, the directions indicate that a cross in the form of a tree is to be seen on stage. (RAE, II, 413-a.) The doctrine of grace

---

[30] Juan Eduardo Cirlot, *Diccionario de símbolos tradicionales* (Barcelona, 1958), 77.

through the eternal repetition of Christ's passion and death is stated in a song by the *músicos* in the shadow of the tree. The symbolism, they explain, is intended to remind the Wife of Christ's death and constitutes, therefore, an elucidation of the mysteries of divine love. The tree itself, to judge from the words of the song, is to represent a poplar: "Veréis como arranco / Un álamo blanco..." (415-a.) The legendary name, "Caballero de Olmedo," I submit, might well have suggested to Lope the model on which he fashioned his protagonist and his conception of the tragic hero.

The traditional symbolism in the dream is central to the substance of the play. The significant elements are the goldfinch, the hawk, the broom bush on which the small bird comes to rest, the almond tree out of which the hawk descends, and the jasmine in which the mate witnesses the sad scene. Herbert Friedmann reduces the complex meaning of the symbolic goldfinch to five related categories.[31] 1) "The goldfinch symbolizes Resurrection." 2) "Associated with the theme of Resurrection after death, but in a minor sense, is the idea of recovery after a serious illness... 3) Immediately united with the theme of Resurrection, however, is the matter of Redemption, and then that of Immortality, towards which Resurrection is the great first step." 4) "The goldfinch symbolizes Sacrifice and especially, the Passion. This was based on the early legend to the effect that while Christ was carrying the cross on the way to Calvary, a little bird fluttered down to His head and pulled out a thorn that was rankling His brow. The sacred blood tinged the feathers of the little creature who has worn the mark ever since." 5) "The goldfinch may symbolize death." (*The Symbolic Goldfinch*, 7-10.) The hawk needs little explanation for it is a bird of prey. It is, therefore, a symbol of destructiveness and stealth.

Far more important is the almond tree which harbors the predator. There was a congeries of meanings of exceedingly long lineage associated with the almond tree. Among others, Covarrubias reports: "Por ser este árbol tan antuviado, el hebreo le llama el velador o madrugador, *saked*, del verbo *sakad*, *vigilare*. Su primera significación es velar y madrugar, ...la palabra *saked*, sinifica

---

[31] Herbert Friedmann, *The Symbolic Goldfinch: Its History and Significance in European Devotional Art* (Washington D. C., 1946).

en su primera sinificación el almendro, y por metáfora el madrugador..." (*Tesoro*, 96-b.) Jobes (*Dictionary*, I, 70.), Arnold Whittick, [32] Fergusson (*Signs*, 31.), Ellacombe (*Plant Lore*, 12.), and Maurice H. Farbridge [33] all concur with the Hebrew etymology, and affirm that the most widely accepted meaning of the almond tree denotes the 'watcher,' the 'awakener,' and, therefore, is a symbol of divine acceptance and approval. John Ingram assigns the same meaning and adds that the early blooming tree also signified haste. [34] A. W. Anderson connects the almond blossom with life after death, and accepts it as a symbol of the immortality of the soul and the resurrection of the spirit. [35] Fergusson calls attention to the relationship between the almond and the *mandorla*, or oblong nimbus (*Signs*, 268.) as does Elizabeth Goldsmith, [36] that commonly surrounds the head of Christ. As a sign of providential watchfulness or vigilance, and permission or sufferance, the almond tree in the dream must be regarded as perhaps the central connotative symbol, because it is precisely this tree that offers shelter to the killer hawk.

The reference to the jasmine tree in which the goldfinch's mate rests is somewhat less precise than its environmental signs. Fergusson regards it as a symbol of the Virgin and amiability. (*Signs*, 40.) Jobes states the same and adds that the jasmine further denotes divine hope, grace, and heavenly felicity because of its star shaped blossom. (*Dictionary*, I, 866.) The meaning of virginity and purity is appropriate to Inés. The love of the two protagonists remains an *amor purus* to the end.

Concerning the broom, I have been relatively unsuccessful in locating material which might shed some light on its symbolic meaning. Charles M. Skinner notes several legends connected with the plant. Because of its dry, sawing noise, when moved by the wind, it was supposed to have lead Judas and the soldiers of Herod to Jesus in the garden of Gethsemane. It was the same

---

[32] Arnold Whittick, *Symbols, Signs, and Their Meaning* (London, 1960), 129.

[33] Maurice H. Farbridge, *Studies in Biblical and Semitic Symbolism* (London, New York, 1923), 26-27.

[34] John Ingram, *Flora Symbolica: Or the Language and Sentiment of Flowers* (London, New York, 1869), 150-151.

[35] A. W. Anderson, *Plants of the Bible* (London, 1956), 19.

[36] Elizabeth Goldsmith, *Sacred Symbols in Art* (New York, 1910), 67.

broom that almost revealed the hiding place of Mary and Jesus when they had taken shelter among them from Herod's officers. "Hence the plant," Skinner writes, "has reason for the humility which its employment for sweeping continues to enforce, and it has additional disgrace in that it was chosen of witches who chose to ride abroad on it at night." [37] It is the broom's identification with betrayal and the witch that Lope may have had in mind.

In Act I, when Alonso describes to Fabia his first glimpse of Inés, he remarks: "Los corales y las perlas / dejó Inés, porque sabía / que las llevaban mejores / los dientes y las mejillas." (794-b.) The coral, especially the pink variety, was regarded from ancient times as an amulet against the disasters of nature, disease, ill-fortune, and sorcery, among other things, Jobes records. (*Dictionary,* I, 370.) In Italy, she continues, it was used for an antidote to counteract the evil eye. The same idea is found in Brand's *Popular Antiquities* (London, 1849), I, 166. Reginald Scot observes, in his *Discovery of Witchcraft,* that the coral "...preserveth such as bear it from fascination or bewitching, and in this respect they are hanged about children's necks." (*Popular Antiquities,* II, 85.) The same anthology records a passage from *Bartholomeus de Proprietatibus Rerum* (1536): "Wytches tell, that this stone withstondeth lyghtenynge. It putteth of lyghtenyng, whirlewynde, tempeste, and stormes fro shippes and houses that it is in. — The red (coral) helpeth ayenst the fendes gyle and scorne..." (*Popular Antiquities,* II, 86.) Inés's leaving her corals at home on this day exposes her to the full range of *maleficium.* [38]

The other article of jewelry the heroine has laid aside, the pearls, is equally interesting in its symbolism and folkloric reference. Fergusson designates the pearl as a sign of salvation, citing Mathew 13:45 and 7:6 (*Signs,* 57.) Covarrubias's remarks on the pearl are unusually cogent: "...y son de mucho provecho en la medicina para passiones y enfermedades del coraçon y celebro... aprovechan a los melancólicos, consumiendo los vapores negros

---

[37] Charles M. Skinner, *Myths and Legends of Flowers, Trees, Fruits, and Plants* (Philadelphia and London, 1911).

[38] The action of Tirso de Molina's *El melancólico* is curiously implicated in a chain or necklace of corals and suspected bewitchment. See especially Acts II and III.

que suben al coraçon y a la cabeça con que se les confusca el resplandor lúcido de sus espíritus." (*Tesoro*, 864-a.) The pearls and the corals, then, which Inés has left behind, are consistent with the substance of the moment when both the hero and heroine are caught up in the initial phases of their truancy. Symbolically viewed, had Inés worn her usual jewelry, perhaps this love might have taken a more traditional direction, one less vulnerable to peril.

The unicorn and the basilisk also figure prominently in the young man's recounting of his first vision of Inés. (795-a.) Besides the traditional association of the unicorn with chastity and purity, Cirlot points out that the horn was representative of the "espada o palabra de Dios," and thus signified Christ and His strength. (*Diccionario*, 416.) The fabulous basilisk, with its poisonous eyes, says Fergusson, was commonly linked with the devil. This interpretation derives from Psalm 91:13. (*Signs*, 41.)

There remains one other symbol of major significance: the phoenix to which Alonso is likened by Tello in the lengthy *relación* at the end of the tragedy. (824-b.) Covarrubias relates the bird to Christ as a harbinger of His death:

> Y assí Plinio, Tácito, como Dión concurren aver visto esta ave en Egipto, siendo cónsules Paulo Fabro y L. Vitellio, que vino a ser un año antes de la muerte de Tiberio, concurriendo con la de nuestro Redentor Jesu Christo y su gloriosíssima Resurrección, de que carecía pronóstico. Algunos autores afirman esto, fundados en la autoridad de los arriba alegados. La consideración es pía y muchos han formado geroglíficos de la fénix, aplicándolos a la Resurrección de nuestro Redentor... (*Tesoro*, 589-a.)

Fergusson (*Signs*, 23.), Cirlot (*Diccionario*, 202.), and Goldsmith (*Sacred Symbols*, 287.) all assign the same meaning. It is perhaps fitting that Lope should bring his tragedy to a close with the metaphor of the phoenix, thus again correlating Christ and Alonso. For it is precisely in the unique union of the goldfinch with the hawk that the new anagogical phoenix is born again, again, and again.

> "For there must be also heresies among you,
> that they which are approved may be made
> manifest among you."
> I Corinthians, 11:19.

BIBLIOGRAPHY

I. BIBLIOGRAPTY OF CITED WORKS

ALONSO, DÁMASO: "Tres procesos de dramatización," in *De los siglos oscuros al de oro*. Madrid, 1958.
AMADOR DE LOS RÍOS, JOSÉ: "De las arte mágicas y de adivinación," *Revista de España*, XVII (1870), 5-17:379-396, XVIII (1871), 5-26:321-348.
ANDERSON, A. W.: *Plants of the Bible*. London, 1956.
ANDERSON-IMBERT, ENRIQUE: "Lope dramatiza un cantar," in *Grandes libros de occidente*. Mexico, 1957.
AUDIAU, J.: *Les quatres troubadours d'Ussel*. Paris, 1922.
BAMBOROUGH, J. B.: *The Little World of Man*. London, 1952.
BATAILLON, MARCEL: *La Célestine selon Fernando de Rojas*. Paris, 1961.
BLECUA, JOSÉ M.: "Nota al Caballero de Olmedo," *Nueva Revista de filología hispánica*, VIII (1954), 190.
BLUMMER, H.: *The Home Life of the Ancient Greeks*. New York, 1893.
BRAND, JOHN: *Observations on the Popular Antiquities of Great Britain*. Arranged, revised, and enlarged by Sir Henry Ellis. 3 volumes. London, 1849.
BRIGHT, TIMOTHY: *A Treatise of Melancholy*. London, 1586.
BURTON, ROBERT: *The Anatomy of Melancholy*. Everyman's Library. London, 1961.
CANAL GÓMEZ, M. (Editor): *Cancionero de Roma*. Volumes II and III of the Biblioteca Hispano-Italiana. Florence, 1935. [Commonly cited as vols. I and II.]
CAPELLANUS, ANDREAS: *The Art of Courtly Love*. Translated by John Jay Parry. New York, 1959.
CARCOPINO, JEROME: *Daily Life in Ancient Rome*. Oxford, England, 1933.
CARO BAROJA, JULIO: *Las brujas y su mundo*. Madrid, 1961.
CASA, FRANK P. "The Dramatic Unity of *El Caballero de Olemedo*," *Neophilologus*, V, 234-43.
CASTAÑEGA, MARTÍN DE: *Tratado de las supersticiones y hechicerías*. Sociedad de Bibliófilos Españoles. Volume XVII. Madrid, 1946.
CASTILLO, HERNANDO DEL (Compiler): *Cancionero general*. Sociedad de Bibliófilos Españoles. Volume XXI: 2 tomes. Madrid, 1882.
CIRAC ESTOPAÑÁN, SEBASTIÁN: *Procesos de hechicerías en la Inquisición de Castilla la Nueva*. Madrid, 1942.
CIRLOT, JUAN EDUARDO: *Diccionario de símbolos tradicionales*. Barcelona, 1958.

CIRUELO, PEDRO: *Reprobación de las supersticiones y hechizerías*. s. l., 1547.
CORTÉS, JERÓNIMO: *Lunario nuevo perpetuo y general y pronostica de los tiempos universales*. Madrid, 1598.
COTARELO Y MORI, EMILIO (Editor): *Colección de entremeses, loas, bailes, jácaras, y mojigangas desde fines del siglo XVI a mediados del XVII*. Nueva Biblioteca de Autores Españoles. Volumes XVII and XVIII. Madrid, 1911.
COVARRUBIAS Y HOROZCO, SEBASTIÁN DE: *Tesoro de la lengua castellana o española*. Barcelona, 1943.
CRUZ, SOR JUANA INÉS DE LA: *Obras completas*. Ed. Alfonso Méndez Plancarte. 2 volumes. Mexico, 1951.
D'ARCY, MARTIN: *The Mind and Heart of Love, Lion and Unicorn. A Study of Eros and Agape*. London, 1954.
DELEITÓ Y PIÑUELA, JOSÉ: *La mala vida en la España de Felipe II*. Madrid, 1948.
DEMONY, ALEXANDER J.: *The Heresy of Courtly Love*. New York, 1947.
DE ROUGEMONT, DENIS: *Love in the Western World*. New York, 1957.
DU LAURENS, ANDRÉ: *A Discourse of the Preservation of the Sight: Of Melancolike Diseases; of Rheumes, and of Old Age*. Translated by Richard Surphlet. London, 1599. Shakespeare Association Facsimiles, No. 15. Oxford, England, 1938.
ELLACOMBE, HENRY N.: *The Plant Lore and Garden Craft of Shakespeare*. London, 1884.
ELYOT, THOMAS: *The Castel of Health*. Scholars Facsimiles and Reprints. New York, 1937.
FARBRIDGE, MAURICE H.: *Studies in Biblical and Semitic Symbolism*. London-New York, 1923.
FERGUSSON, GEORGE: *Signs and Symbols in Christian Art*. New York, 1954.
FERRAND, JACQUES: *Erotomania, Or a Treatise Discoursing of the Essence, Causes, Symptomes, Prognostics, and Cure of Love or Erotic Melancholy*. Translated by Edmund Chilmead. Oxford, 1640.
FITA, FIDEL: "El Caballero de Olmedo y la Orden de Santiago," *Boletín de la Real Academia de la Historia*, XLVI (1905), 398-422.
FOULCHÉ-DELBOSC, R. (Editor): *Cancionero castellano del siglo XV*. Nueva Biblioteca de Autores Españoles. Volumes XIX and XXII. [Commonly cited as vols. I and II.]
FRIEDMANN, HERBERT: *The Symbolic Goldfinch: Its History and Significance in European Devotional Art*. Washington D. C., 1946.
GERARD, ALBERT:"Baroque Unity and the Dualities of *El Caballero de Olmedo,*" *Romanic Review*, LVI, 92-106.
GILLET, JOSEPH E.: *'Propalladia' and Other Works*. 4 volumes. Bryn Mawr, 1943.
GOLDSMITH, ELIZABETH: *Sacred Symbols in Art*. New York, 1910.
GÓMEZ DE LA SERNA, RAMÓN: "El Caballero de Olmedo," *Revista cubana*, XIV (1940), 38-55.
GRANADA, FRAY LUIS DE: *Introducción del símbolo de la fe*. In *Obras*. Ed. Fray Justo Cuervo. Volumes V-IX. Madrid, 1908.
GREEN, OTIS H.: *Spain and the Western Tradition*. 2 volumes. Madison, Wisconsin, 1963-1964.
HANSEN, JOSEPH: *Zauberwahn, Inquisition, und Hexenprozess im Mittelalter und die Enstehung der grossen Hexenverfolgung*. München-Leipzig,1900.
HESSE, EVERETT W. "The Role of the Mind in Lope's *El Caballero de Olmedo,"Symposium*, XIX, 58-66.

HOLE, CHRISTINE: *A Mirror of Witchcraft.* London, 1957.
HUARTE DE SAN JUAN, JUAN: *Examen de ingenios para las ciencias.* Ed. R. Sanz. Madrid, 1930.
HUNT, MORTON M.: *The Natural History of Love.* New York, 1959.
HUXLEY, ALDOUS: *The Devils of Loudun.* New York, 1952.
INGRAM, JOHN: *Flora Symbolica: Or the Language and Sentiment of Flowers.* London-New York, 1869.
JOBES, GERTRUDE: *A Dictionary of Mythology, Folklore, and Symbols.* 3 volumes. New York, 1961.
JONES, W. H. S.: *Greek Morality.* London, 1906 .
JULIÁ MARTÍNEZ, EDUARDO (Editor): *Comedia del Caballero de Olmedo.* Edition and prologue. Madrid, 1944.
KRAMER, HENRY, and SPRENGER, JOSEPH: *Malleus maleficarum.* Translated by Montague Summers. London, 1951.
LAGUNA, ANDRÉS: Translation and commentaries to Pedacio Dioscórides, *Acerca de la materia medicinal y de los venenos mortíferos.* Amberes, 1555.
LANG, HENRY R. (Editor): *Cancionero gallego-castelhano.* New York, 1902.
LAVATER, LEWES: *Of Ghostes and Spirites Walking by Nyght.* Translated by R. H. London, 1572. Facsimile edition by J. Dover Wilson and May Yardley. Oxford, England, 1929.
LEA, HENRY CHARLES: *A History of the Inquisition of Spain.* 4 volumes. New York, 1907.
———: *Materials Towards a History of Witchcraft.* 3 volumes. Philadelphia, 1939.
LEÓN, FRAY LUIS DE: *Obras completas.* Ed. P. Félix García, O. S. A. Madrid, 1951.
———: *La perfecta casada.* In *Obras completas.*
LEYES, JACOBO DE LAS: *Flores de las leyes.* In *Memorial histórico español.* Ed. Real Academia de la Historia. Volume II. Madrid, 1851.
LOCKE, FREDERICK (Editor): "Introduction" to Andreas Capellanus, *The Art of Courtly Love.* Translated by John Jay Parry and abridged by Frederick Locke. New York, 1957.
MACDONALD, INEZ: *El Caballero de Olmedo.* Edition and notes. Cambridge, England, 1935.
———: "Why Lope?" *Bulletin of Spanish Studies,* XII (1935), 185-197.
MADRIGAL, ALFONSO DE (EL TOSTADO): *Tractado por el qual se prueba por la Santa Escriptura como al ome es necessario amar, é el que verdaderamente ama es necessario que se turbe.* Sociedad de Bibliófilos Españoles, Volume XXIX. Madrid, 1892.
MARÍN, DIEGO: "La ambigüedad poética en *El Caballero de Olmedo*," *Hispanófila,* XXIV, 1-11.
MCCRARY, WILLIAM C.: "*Fuenteovejuna*: Its Platonic Conception and Execution," *Studies in Philology,* LVIII (1961), 179-192.
———: "La elaboración de una escena simbológica de Tirso de Molina," *Hispanófila,* XIII (1961), 23-32.
MENÉNDEZ Y PELAYO, MARCELINO: *Historia de los heterodoxos españoles.* 8 volumes. Santander, 1947. [Volumes 35-42 of *Obras completas,* ed. Enrique Sánchez Reyes.]
NAVARRO, GASPAR: *Tribunal de superstición ladina.* Huesca, 1631.
NIGG, WALTER: *The Heretics.* Translated by Richard and Clara Winston. New York, 1962.
PARKER, ALEXANDER A.: "The Approach to the Spanish Golden Age Drama," *Tulane Drama Review,* IV (1959), 42-59.

PLINIUS, CAIUS: *The Natural History.* Translated by John Bostock and H. T. Riley. 6 volumes. London, 1857.

QUEVEDO Y VILLEGAS, FRANCISCO: *Obras en prosa.* Ed. Luis Astrana Marín. Madrid, 1932.

QUIÑONES BENAVENTE, JUAN DE: *Tratado de las langostas.* Madrid, 1619.

RÍO, MARTÍN DEL: *Disquisitionum magicarum libri sex.* Venice, 1616.

ROMERO Y GILSANZ, F.: "El Caballero de Olmedo," *Revista contemporánea,* CVII (1897), 82-102.

SALAZAR Y FRÍAS, ADOLFO DE: *Relacion y epilogo de lo que a resultado de la visita q hizo el sancto Offi° en las montañas de Navarra y otras partes con el hedito de gracia concedido a los que ouiesen ycurrido en la secta de Brujos conforme a las relaciones que de todo ello se an Remitido al Consejo.* In *Anuario de Ausko-Folklore,* XII, 115-130.

FERNÁNDEZ DE SAN PEDRO, DIEGO: *Sermón de amor.* In Menéndez y Pelayo, Marcelino. *Orígenes de la novela.* Nueva Biblioteca de Autores Españoles. Volume VII. Madrid, 1907.

————: *Cárcel de amor.* In *Orígenes de la novela.* Volume VII.

SARRAILH, JEAN: *El Caballero de Olmedo.* Edition and prologue. Paris, 1935.

SEDEÑO DE MESA, ALONSO MANUEL: *Traducción de los aphorismos de Hipócrates.* Madrid, 1699.

SKINNER, CHARLES M.: *Myths and Legends of Flowers, Trees, Fruits, and Plants.* Philadelphia, 1911.

SOONS, C. A.: "Towards an Interpretation of *El Caballero de Olmedo*," *Romanische Forschungen,* LXXIII (1961), 160-168.

SPITZER, LEO: *L'amour lointain de Jaufré Rudel et la poesie des troubadours.* University of North Carolina Studies in the Romance Languages and Literatures. Chapel Hill, 1944.

SUMMERS, MONTAGUE: *The History of Witchcraft.* New York, 1956.

TORNER, FLORENCIO M.: *Doña Oliva Sabuco de Nantes.* Madrid, 1935.

TURNER, ALISON: "The Dramatic Function of Imagery and Symbolism in *Peribáñez* and *El Caballero de Olmedo,*" *"Symposium,* XX, 174-186.

VALENCY, MAURICE: *In Praise of Love.* New York, 1958.

VELÁZQUEZ, ANDRÉS: *Libro de la melancolía.* Sevilla, 1585.

VENDRELL Y MILLÁS, FRANCISCA (Editor): *Cancionero de palacio.* Barcelona, 1945.

VENEGAS, ALEXO: *Agonía del tránsito de la muerte con los avisos y consuelos que cerca della son provechosas.* Nueva Biblioteca de Autores Españoles. Volume XVI. Madrid, 1911.

VIVES, JUAN LUIS: *Obras completas.* Ed. Lorenzo Riber. 2 volumes. Madrid, 1947.

————: *Formación de la mujer cristiana.* In *Obras completas,* I.

————: *Tratado del alma.* In *Obras completas,* I.

WHITTICK, ARNOLD: *Symbols, Signs, and Their Meaning.* London, 1960.

WIND, EDGAR: *Pagan Mysteries in the Renaissance.* London, 1958.

YATES, DONALD A.: "The Poetry of the Fantastic in *El Caballero de Olmedo,*" *Hispania,* XLIII (1960), 503-507.

II. OTHER USEFUL MATERIALS NOT CITED ELSEWHERE

ALBARRACÍN TEULON, AGUSTÍN: *La medicina en el teatro de Lope de Vega.* Madrid, 1954.

BABB, LAWRENCE: "The Psychological Conception of Love in the Elizabethan and Early Tudor Drama," *Publications of the Modern Language Associa-*

tion, LVI (1941), 1020-1035.

———: *The Elizabethan Malady*. East Lansing, Michigan, 1951.

BAXTER, RICHARD: *The Certainty of the World of Spirites*. London, 1691.

BAYLEY, HAROLD: *The Lost Language of Symbolism*. London, 1952.

BERNDT, ERNA RUTH: *Amor, muerte, y fortuna en 'la Celestina.'* Madrid, 1963.

BONILLA, LUIS: *Historia de la hechicería y de las brujas*. Madrid, 1962.

BOVET, RICHARD: *Pandemonium*. [1684] Aldington, Kent, 1951.

BRIGGS, KATHERINE MARY: *Pale Hecate's Team*. London, 1962.

CARRANZA, FRAY BARTOLOMÉ: *Controversias teológicas*. Rome, 1546.

CORTÉS, JERÓNIMO: *Secretos de la naturaleza*. Barcelona, 1582.

———: *Libro de phisonomía natural*. Alcalá de Henares, 1607.

———: *Fisonomía y varios secretos de la naturaleza*. s. l., s. f.

ESCUDERO ORTUÑO, ALBERTO: *Concepto de la melancolía en el siglo XVII*. Huesca, 1950.

GRANADA, FRAY LUIS DE: *Memorial de la vida cristiana*. In *Obras*. Ed. Fray Justo Cuervo. Volume III. Madrid, 1908.

GREEN, OTIS H.: "Courtly Love in the Spanish Cancioneros," *Publications of the Modern Language Association*, LXIV (1949) 247-301.

———: *El amor cortés en Quevedo*. Zaragoza, 1955.

HALSTEAD, FRANK G.: "The Optics of Love: Notes on a Concept of Atomistic Philosophy in the Theater of Tirso de Molina," *Publications of the Modern Language Association*, LVIII (1943), 108-121.

HOPKIN, CHARLES EDWARD: *The Share of Thomas Aquinas in the Growth of the Witchcraft Delusion*. Philadelphia, 1940.

HUGHES, PENNETHORNE: *Witchcraft*. London, 1952.

LELAND, CHARLES: *Arcadia or the Gospel of the Witches*. London, 1899.

LEMNE, LEVIN [LEVINUS LEMNIUS]: *Les occultes merveilles et secretz de nature*. Paris, 1574.

LETHBRIDGE, THOMAS CHARLES: *Witches: Investigating an Ancient Religion*. London, 1962.

LÓPE DE VEGA, ANTONIO: *Paradoxas racionales*. Ed. E. Buceta. Madrid, 1935.

LÓPEZ GÓMEZ, QUINTÍN: *Magia goética, artes infernales y medios seguros para prevenirlas y contrarrestarlas*. Barcelona, 1914.

LOWES, JOHN L.: "The Loveres Maladye of Hereos," *Modern Philology*, XI (1913-14), 491-456.

MAPLE, ERIC: *The Dark World of Witches*. London, 1962.

MURRAY, MARGARET: *The God of the Witches*. New York, 1952.

RAMÍREZ DE CARRIÓN, MANUEL: *Maravillas de la naturaleza*. Córdoba, 1629.

RIQUER, MARTÍN DE: *La lírica de los trovadores*. Barcelona, 1948.

ROBBINS, RUSSEL H.: *Encyclopedia of Witchcraft and Demonology*. New York, 1959.

SCOT, REGINALD: *The Discoverie of Witchcraft*. London, 1584.

THOMPSON, RICHARD L.: *A History of the Devil*. London, 1929.

THORNDIKE, LYNN: *History of Magic and Experimental Science*. 2 volumes. New York, 1929.

TORRE, ALFONSO DE: *Visión delectable de la filosofía y artes liberales*. Biblioteca de Autores Españoles. Vol. XXXVI. Madrid, 1855.

TURMEL, JOSEPH: *The Life of the Devil*. New York, 1930.

WATERS, CLARA E.: *A Handbook of Christian Symbols*. Boston, 1886.

WHYTE, LANCELOT LAW: *The Unconscious before Freud*. London, 1963.

WILLIAMS, CHARLES: *Witchcraft*. London, 1941.

ZILBOORG, GREGORY: *The Medical Man and the Witch*. Baltimore, 1935.

A Note to the Second Printing

The first printing of my study, *The Goldfinch and the Hawk*, appeared in late 1966. I wish to acknowledge my gratitude to those students of the *comedia* whose continuing demand for my essay has prompted a supplementary release. I am indebted to the Editorial Board of the University of North Carolina Studies in the Romance Languages and Literatures, and especially to Professors Urban T. Holmes, Frederick W. Vogler, and George B. Daniel, who have urged me to authorize another issue. Their confidence in the appeal of my monograph to the general public is deeply gratifying and flattering. Having read the study anew, now at greater distance and with less personal involvement, I find that, were I preparing a second edition, I would not substantially alter the argument of the book. I would insist less on some points, perhaps, and modify and rectify others by the addition of material gleaned from subsequent readings and the comments and observations provided by those who have read the analysis with care.

The following brief addendum is offered as additional information in support of the foregoing study. If it clarifies several issues, which to some readers were problematic and difficult ones, its inclusion will be justified. Of concern here are two related questions: first, Lope's unwillingness to attach an undeniable causative value to Fabia's role; and, second, his subtle and unobtrusive, albeit empirically demonstrable, shaping of Alonso's image in such a way that the memory of Christ is evoked. I shall make reference throughout to the two part tragedy *Próspera* and *Adversa fortuna de don Alvaro de Luna*,[1] which in some ways displays a kindred conception of the tragic art.

The fall of Rodrigo from his horse at the beginning of Act III is crucial to the mechanics of Lope's tragedy, for it is because of this misfortune that Rodrigo discovers the identity of his competitor beyond the shadow of a doubt. Lope's arrangement of scenes at this point *suggests* that Rodrigo's disgrace and Alonso's success are in some way related to Fabia's hellish plan. But the dramatist *only* suggests. He leaves any specific indictment of the *tercera* as a causative agent to the spectator's powers of inference, as he has done throughout the play. The point is that Lope has meticulously coordinated dramatic event, scene disposition, and the comments of his characters in such a way that the spectacle invites the audience to distinguish between plot and action, character and role, and to assign to Fabia's character the role of a malefactress. Given the corpus of the contemporary belief about witches, Fabia's instrumentality in this fatal moment need not be stated explicitly. That the *mosqueteros* might have seen in this episode, and probably did, a sinister intercession is an hypothesis which appears to receive considerable support from the *Próspera fortuna*.

At the beginning of Act III (1882 a-b.) we are witness to a royal joust celebrating the coronation of Juan II. The scene is remarkably similar to Lope's initiation of his third *jornada*. It is here in Tirso's play that John's utter dependence on Alvaro becomes clear. The young favorite is unseated in the contest, an unexpected event which so disturbs the Monarch that he leaves the royal box to rush to his friend's side. Pablillos explains the mishap as the work of a deceitful old hag: "Alguna vieja bellaca/ de mal ojo le miró:/ ¿por qué aquella que llegó/ a cuarenta, no se saca los ojos por no matar?" (1882-b.) The *gracioso* would well have understood Fabia's comment: "¿Qué yo tus hazañas causo?/ Basta, que no lo sabía."

If Lope has elected only to insinuate Fabia's shadow into the fabric of his tragedy, this hesitation to lay full and total responsibility for all that transpires squarely at her threshold is due to several factors. Theoretically such an attachment of guilt would be heretical—the *Malleus* and common opinion notwithstanding. But of greater importance to our inquiry is the logic of a Christian tragedy. To begin with, tragedy in general, ancient or modern, cannot suffer the presence of villains to whom all calamity can be conveniently imputed. A villain of necessity requires a victim whose utter innocence defines the very identity of the villain. And such an abundance of innocence brings with it two effects that are antagonistic to tragedy: the hero's catastrophe would render him pathetic, worthy of our sorrow, commiseration, etc.; and, secondly, excessive innocence excludes a personal involvement of the hero in a moral action. He would be fatally deprived of all responsibility for his behavior. The villain-victim polarity describes melodrama, not tragedy. Perhaps more than any other characteristic, tragedy exalts objectivity. Unlike melodrama or high social drama, the tragic art remains nonpartisan in its outlook.

The creation of effective tragedy within a Christian consciousness does not alter this logic. On the contrary, the doctrines of the Fall of Man, free will, a divinely ordered nature, and a loving and merciful God, so supremely concerned with his creation and man's redemption that "He gave His only begotten son," constitute a metaphysical and theodiceal frame of reference singularly inviting to tragedy's purposes. Subsequent to the Fall, man's intelligence was reduced to but a shadow of its former status. As Calderón has so effectively dramatized in the *autos*, *La vida es sueño*, post-Eden Adam was afflicted with the burden of original sin and death. In short, he acquired all of his terrestrial limitations. From Paradise, however, he took freedom of choice with him and went forth into a nature no longer friendly and subservient, but rather capricious and frequently hostile. It was a world created by God to be a theater in which all things had purpose and place. Thomas's remark, "Deus et natura nihil frustra faciunt," most aptly describes this universe into which man was cast. What is important here is man's limitations, his free will, and a natural order in which all objects and events have a reference. For the Christian tragedian of the Renaissance, this tradition provided an image of man as imperfect, therefore subject to error, but capable of redemption and of attaining higher truths. In so far as man was not cut off from redemption, therefore, God's continuing love was made manifest.

Now if we compare Lope's tragedy to this world view, certain problems related to Fabia and Alonso will present fewer difficulties. In a natural order so structured it follows that all causality—ultimately—resides either in the human bosom or the Divine Intelligence. Because of man's *albedrío*, Alonso's passion is, in the final accounting, his own responsibility. Yet this posture makes the young hero into a crass trangressor—a villain. Fabia's presence, then, serves as an efficient mitigating factor. She assumes a causal denomination in so far as her skills aid and abet the tragic action. This is why Lope casts her shadow over the plot throughout, but stops short of designating her as a causal agent *per se*. Fabia cooperates with nature; that is her function and her place in an order which assigns her a role to play, *Dei permissu*. Her causality, then, must be understood as instrumental, a secondary rather than primary causality. Alonso's departure from life has its beginnings in his own illicit passion. Nature allows passion, but she also suffers a witch. Through Fabia Lope can focus on his hero's blindness and limitations, and because of her instrumentality in the action, Alonso can come to understand the relationship between transgression, human imperfection, and man's continuing dependence on God—which is the higher truth. Significantly, therefore, the hero's *anagnorisis* takes the form of a confession in which no mention is made of the *alcahueta*. All of that is past at this point in the action. The dying hero cannot blame Fabia: to do so would be to fall into a partisan posture and the tragedy would compromise its objectivity.

Ruy López's response to his disgrace is the same as that of Alonso. The fallen Regent realizes that Gracía—his Judas—acted only as the 'whip' of God: "¿Esto dije? No lo hiciera (.e., punish his servant)/ que el azote a Dios quitara/ du su mano./ No en balde fué mi enemigo;/ Dios castiga mi pecado./ Instrumento/ fue el traidor de mi castigo;/ . . . / . . . y aunque apriesa,/ destas pompas he caido,/ si Dios la da y las quita, [sic] / no me pesa." (1887-b.) Lope's hero is brief because brevity is forced upon him by imminent death. He goes straight to the point and makes his peace with God. Ruy can afford to be more analytical and philosophical in his theodicy: unlike Alonso, he is not looking into the face of eternity. Both men share, nonetheless, a common insight.

Alonso's last utterances return the hero's errant spirit to its Maker. He recognizes nature as deceptive, his own part in his downfall, and begs God's forgiveness. In essence he cries, "Father, forgive me, for I knew not what I did." In the end Alonso is crucified on the cross of his own humanity. It should not be surprising, therefore, that in the *Caballero* Lope should have delicately compared the image of the tragic hero to the broad outlines of the life of Jesus. He was not alone in drawing forth this analogy. In the *Próspera fortuna*, Ruy López also lickens himself to Christ; "¿Cómo, si la culpa es mia,/ a Cristo parezco yo,/ que siendo Dios, le vendío/ el que en su plato comía?" (1887-a.) The distant similarity between Jesus and Ruy is made even more precise by García's betrayal of his master and Ruy's fall after thirty two years of service to his Monarch. In the second play of the duo history repeats itself. Not only does Alvaro's tragedy repeat the design of his predecessor, but the dramatist again provides his spectator with sufficient detail to stimulate the recall of Christ's suffering and agony in bearing His cross. Alvaro served his Sovereign for thirty two years, as Christs' mission on earth was ended in his thirty third year, having served for thirty two. The Constable's career inflamed the jealousies of the nobility which eventually plotted and demanded his death, an event which to the play's author recapitulates the envy and suspicions of the chief priests during the life of Christ. Perhaps the most striking detail occurs when the secretary visits the imprisoned and enchained Alvaro to inform him of his death sentence. Alvaro cries for water: "Un jarro de agua me trae;/ porque siento con desmayo/ esta sentencia, este rayo/ que del mismo cielo cae. . ." (1935-b.) One cannot but be reminded of Jesus's agonizing last words as recorded in John 19:28: "After this, Jesus, knowing that all was now finished, said (to fulfil the prophecy), 'I thirst.' . . . When Jesus had received the vinegar, he said, 'It is finished'; and he bowed his head and gave up his spirit." After the momentary shock, Alvaro also realizes that "it is finished," and that his life will be forever an example of the irony of the human condition: "Bien sé que atalaya soy/ que subí desde la cuna/ al monte de la fortuna, ..." (1936-a.) If he has had to bear the indignities of being an unpopular *privado*, he can at least take comfort in knowing that his misfortunes are visited upon him by heaven as part of a grander plan in which his role is to be that of the chosen vessel: "Los mismos cielos envían/ a un magnánimo este mal/ para ejemplo universal/ de los hombres que confían/ en los hombres, y si vengo/ a ser ejemplo del mundo,/ aun cayendo en lo profundo/ hoy singular dicha tengo." (1929-a.)

It is hoped that the foregoing comparisons have established that Lope was not unique in relating tragedy to a theodiceal view. In all three plays the protagonists are treated as elected men whose images are referred to the archetypal construct of Christ's passion. This referral, I submit, in no way implies that Christ is a tragic figure. Conversely, the referral does not make Christ figures of the three heroes. In so far, however, as their respective tragedies re-enact events and circumstances similar to those of Jesus's life, the three tragic protagonists become 'Christomimetic.' The conception of the tragic hero as a *Christomimetes* has its origin, I believe, in the understanding of Jesus as the perfect *man*, and hence a model against which to measure and assess the actions of an elected individual whose life inperfectly recapitulates that of Christ. The model, then, confers Christian significance and reference on the tragic figure. If in death the humanity of the Son of Man was affirmed and the Father's love for humankind announced once and for all, how much more redemptive and reconciling are the fall and decease of the tragic hero when experienced as sacramental of that sacrifice and all it proclaimed?

The University of Kentucky   June, 1968
Lexington, Kentucky

Notes

1. The authorship of these plays has been a matter of dispute. Both Tirso de Molina and Mira de Amescua have been put forward as possible authors. For the sake of convenience I shall refer to Tirso as the author. All references are to Tirso de Molina, *Obras dramáticas completas,* ed. Blanca de los Ríos (Madrid, 1946), I, pp. 1857-93, 1900-37.

www.ingramcontent.com/pod-product-compliance
Lightning Source LLC
Chambersburg PA
CBHW021843220426
43663CB00005B/375